Tabitha Brown's Western Adventures

A GRANDMOTHER'S ACCOUNT OF HER TREK
FROM MISSOURI TO OREGON
(1846–1858)

. *A Sequel to*
CLARK AND TABITHA BROWN

by Ella Brown Spooner

Illustrated

EXPOSITION PRESS
New York

Exposition Press Inc.. 386 Fourth Avenue, New York 16, N.Y.

FIRST EDITION

ELLA BROWN SPOONER

Contents

TABITHA BROWN'S
WESTERN ADVENTURES

We Traveled With Them

IN THE PRECEDING VOLUME we went along with Clark and Tabitha Brown. We joined with them in their adventures, attended their wedding in the meetinghouse, and followed them from Massachusetts to Vermont and then to New Hampshire. We had a share in stormy scenes—whether unbelievably ridiculous or equally tragic. Also, we shall long remember that we witnessed tender sympathy and days of heartwarming human happiness.

There was history in the making. Then, suddenly, before our eyes, the Browns were transplanted to Maryland, near Washington. There, according to Tabitha, they found supreme happiness with their three young children, her mother, Lois Haynes Moffatt, and his brother Captain John Brown.

But evidently the Good Lord had other plans for Tabitha Brown, for within the next two years the Reverend Clark Brown had gone to his long home, and his body had been laid to rest near the altar of his church. As the parish did not call another minister for quite a while, Mrs. Brown was left in possession of the *glebe*, as it was called. This is the manse that was being built while the family waited in Washington, and was entertained in the mansion at Mount Vernon.

Both Tabitha's mother and Captain John Brown had personal property. We know that Mrs. Brown was not left penniless, as the Browns had owned the spacious New Hampshire home, and besides there is mention of inherited land in Pennsylvania and New York State. According to family records, Mrs. Brown conducted a school for girls from the time of her husband's passing until she left Maryland.

It was after the passing of Mr. Brown in 1817 that Francis Scott Key, a family friend, came and checked over the store

9

of sermons. He selected a number of them and had them published in 1819.

Again surprising events seemed to pursue Tabitha Brown. In a few years she had yielded to the pleadings of her sons and had purchased a sloop, allowing them to go to sea. They would imitate the exploits of Uncle John and would have a clipper ship! The boys had a shipwrecking experience off the rocky coast of New England. They were rescued and returned home very much crestfallen.

It was then that Mrs. Brown, taking prompt advantage of their meek and lowly state of mind, persuaded them to go inland as far as possible from the sea and boats! Hence, in the year 1824, we find the Browns living in St. Charles, near St. Louis. The two sons had learned to till the soil and support their families on nearby land; the daughter Pherne, had been invited to bring her young husband and make a home for Captain John Brown in a house he had purchased in St. Charles, which they did.

"The fleeting hours are slipping swiftly by. . . ." So said Clark Brown about 1800. We may observe that it seems true today, as it doubtless did for these younger Browns living by the Mississippi; for it was only a few brief years until they were nearing thirty and there were grandchildren.

The second son, Manthano, left the group and settled on four hundred acres near Kansas City. There he had a nearly independent economic unit. Supplies from corn and wheat to sheep were raised on his land; spinning wheels were busy and so were shoemakers in his shop, turning out boots and shoes for market. Writing to his mother in 1836, he said, "If my old place on Sharrette Creek is worth $1,000, my place here is better worth $10,000. We are well and satisfied. . . . I live in perfect peace."

We may interject here that there did come a time during those heartbreaking years of the War Between the States when he was in anything but peace; when the people of his state were being overrun by one faction or the other—intruders searching for plunder in a border state. Then came those soul-trying years of reconstruction that had very much concerned him and his sons

Franklin and Thomas Clark, both druggists in nearby towns.

Here we note that Manthano, second son of Clark and Tabitha, born in the year 1802 in the Elm Tree House in Brimfield, Massachusetts, lived until 1876. His wife, Sarah Lawrence Hamilton Brown, survived him twenty-five years. She was from Stanford, Kentucky, the daughter of Thomas and Rachel (Crow) Hamilton of Stanford-Danville.

Also we find the elder brother, Orus, eagerly listening to stories of the western wonderland and deciding to do his own exploring. Could these glowing accounts be true? The old wanderlust returned. In 1843 he and several others crossed the plains successfully in three months' time on horseback and with packhorses, following the Columbia River to Portland, and the Willamette up to Salem; then on to Forest Grove. There he stayed over a year to test the soil. During the winter he accompanied one of General John C. Fremont's expeditions in search for a pass through the Cascade Mountains. On the return journey across the plains the men were sometimes in ludicrous situations and then, in situations not so much so, they nearly perished.

Orus reported that he had found "Paradise." He enthusiastically persuaded his mother, sister, and uncle John to dispose of worldly goods and make preparations for an early start in the spring of 1846. This they did.

In some parts of the Midwest there was a saying, "The bottom has dropped out of the roads," referring, of course, to the miry clay in the month of March. Those were the damp and dreary days with streams of rain on the windowpane or gushing from the big rain barrel or filling the cistern under the porch. The family was really house-tied and men were using hip-length boots. Then came the time of drying clay, and mid-April brought release—new life and hopes and plans.

So it was with our Pilgrims. After much preparation the previous year, small wonder that April 15, 1846, was to them the great date of history!

The long-awaited day arrived and soon they were in a train of wagons. After bidding farewell forever to kith and kin, they were hopefully "setting sail in prairie schooners." They brought

11

along some members of the family of *Equidae* and quite a number of needed kine. These matters having been arranged, and the *impedimenta* brought up (not to any front-line trenches) . . . to the last of the frontier lines, they then departed for the uttermost parts of "Paradise."

Introduction for Brimfield Heroine Letter

During Orus Brown's "inspection tour," when he had stayed over in '44, it so happened that the winter was mild and rather inviting for travelers. Our Pilgrims, therefore, had been in high spirits and hoped to arrive in three months, as Orus had done. But fate had intervened. It brought them a winter unusually cold, a guide who led them astray and various other happenings.

After a few years, when Mrs. Brown had been well settled, she was jubilant over their success. She then wrote the story of their most thrilling adventures.

We now attend her narration (given in her own words).

The Brimfield Heroine Letter

Forest Grove, West Tualatin Plain
Washington County
Oregon Territory
August, 1854.

MY DEAR BROTHER AND SISTER:

It is impossible for me to express to you the unspeakable pleasure and happiness your letter of the 29th of June gave me yesterday. Not hearing from you for so great a length of time, I had concluded myself to be the last one of my father's family remaining here, a pilgrim in the wide world to complete the work that God intended me to do.

Oh, that I could be present with you and Margaret, and relate in the hearing of your children the numerous vicissitudes

12

and dangers I have encountered by land and sea since I last parted from you and Margaret in Brimfield. It would fill a volume of many pages, but I will give a few items from the time I left Missouri in April, 1846, for Oregon.

I expected all three of my children to accompany me, but Manthano was detained by sickness, and his wife was unwilling to leave her parents.

I provided for myself a good ox-wagon team, a good supply of what was requisite for the comfort of myself, Captain Brown, and my driver, for Uncle John insisted on coming and crossed the plains on horseback. Orus Brown with wife and eight children, Virgil Pringle, Pherne's husband with wife and five children, fitted out their separate families and joined a train of forty more for Oregon in high expectations of gaining the wished-for land of promise.

The novelty of our journey, with a few exceptions, was pleasing and prosperous until after we passed Fort Hall. Then we were within six hundred miles of Oregon City, if we had kept the old road down the Columbia River. But three or four trains of emigrants were decoyed off by a rascally fellow, who came out from the settlement in Oregon, assuring us that he had found a near cut-off; that if we would follow him, we would be in the settlement long before those who had gone down the Columbia.

This was in August. The idea of shortening a long journey caused us to yield to his advice. Our sufferings from that time no tongue can tell. (He left a pilot with us who proved to be an excellent man; otherwise, we never would have seen Oregon.) He said he would clear the road before us; that we should have no trouble in rolling our wagons after him. He robbed us of what he could by lying; and left us to the depredations of Indians, wild beasts, and starvation. But God was with us.

We had sixty miles of desert without grass or water, mountains to climb, cattle giving out, wagons breaking, emigrants sick and dying, hostile Indians to guard against by night and by day to keep from being killed, or having our horses and cattle arrowed or stolen.

We were carried south of Oregon hundreds of miles into

13

Utah Territory and California; fell in with the Clamotte, or Klamath, Indians, and Rogue River Indians; lost nearly all of our cattle; passed the Umpquah Mountains twelve miles through. I rode through in three days at the risk of my life, having lost my wagon and all I had but the horse I was on.

Our family was the first that started into the canyon; so we got through much better than those who came after. But of hundreds of wagons, only one came through the canyon without breaking. The canyon was strewn with dead cattle, broken wagons, beds, clothing, and everything but provisions, of which we were nearly destitute. Some people were in the canyon two and three weeks before they could get through; some died without any warning from fatigue and starvation; others ate of the flesh of the cattle that were lying dead by the wayside. After struggling through mud, rocks, and water up to our horses' sides in crossing through this twelve-mile mountain, we opened into the beautiful Umpquah Valley inhabited only by Indians and wild beasts.

We had still another mountain to cross, the Calipoose, besides many miles through mud, snow, rain, and hail.

Winter had set in. We were yet a long distance from any white settlement. The word was "Fly, everyone who can, from starvation"—all not compelled to stay by the cattle to recruit them for further traveling. Mr. Pringle and Pherne insisted on my going ahead with their Uncle John, and trying to save our own lives. They were obliged to stay back for a few days to recruit their worn-out cattle. They divided their last bit of bacon, of which I had three slices, and a teacupful of tea—the last division of all we had. No bread.

We saddled our horses and set off, not knowing that we should ever see each other again. Captain Brown was too old and feeble to render any assistance or protection to me. I was obliged to ride ahead as a pilot, hoping to overtake four or five wagons that left camp the day before. Near sunset we came up with two families that left camp that morning. They had nothing to eat and their cattle had given out. We camped in an oak grove together for the night. In the morning, I divided my last morsel with them, and left them to take care of themselves.

14

I hurried Captain Brown to ride fast so as to overtake the wagons ahead. We passed through beautiful valleys and over high hills; saw but two Indians at a distance through the day. In the after part of the day, Captain Brown complained of sickness, and could only walk his horse at a distance behind mine. He had a swimming in his head and a pain in his stomach. About two or three hours by sun, he became delirious and fell from his horse. I was afraid to jump down from my horse to assist him, as it was one that a woman had never ridden before. He tried to raise himself up on his feet, but could not. I rode close to him and set the end of his *lignum vitae* cane that I had in my hand hard into the ground for him to pull up by. I then urged him to walk a little. He tottered along a few yards and gave out. I then saw a little sunken spot a few steps from me and led his horse down into it. With much difficulty, I got him once more raised on his horse. I then requested him to hold fast by the saddle and horse's mane, and I would lead by bridle. Two miles ahead was another mountain to climb over. As I reached the foot of it, he was able to take the bridle into his own hand, and we passed safely over into a large valley—a wide, extensive, solitary place, and no wagons in sight!

The sun was now setting, the wind was blowing, and the rain was drifting upon the side of the distant mountain. Poor me! I crossed the plain to where three mountain spurs met. Ravines betwixt the points.

Here the shades of night were gathering fast, and I could see the wagon tracks no farther. I alighted from my horse, flung off my saddle and saddlebags, and tied him fast with a lasso rope to a tree. The Captain asked what I was going to do. My answer was, "I am going to camp for the night." He gave a groan and fell to the ground. I gathered my wagon sheet that I had put under my saddle, flung it over a firm projecting limb of a tree, and made me a fine tent. I then stripped the Captain's horse, and tied it; placed saddles, blankets, bridles, etc., under the tent; then helped up the bewildered old gentleman, and introduced him to his new lodgings upon the naked ground. His senses were gone. I covered him as well as I could with blankets,

15

and then seated myself upon my feet behind him, expecting he would be a corpse before morning.

Pause for a moment and consider my situation: worse than alone in a strange wilderness; without food, without fire; cold and shivering; wolves fighting and howling all around me; the darkness of night forbade the stars to shine upon me; solitary— all was solitary as death—but the same Kind Providence that ever has been was watching over me still. I committed my all to Him and felt no fear.

As soon as daylight dawned, I pulled down my tent and saddled the horses. I found the Captain so as to stand upon his feet.

Just at this moment, one of the emigrants that I was trying to overtake came to me. He was in search of venison.

Within eight or ten feet of where my tent had been set, fresh tracks of two Indians were plain to be seen, but I did not know they were there. They had killed and robbed Mr. Newton, but a short distance off, but would not kill his wife because she was a woman. The Indians killed another man on our cut-off; the rest of the emigrants escaped with their lives.

We then traveled on and in a few days came to the foot of the Calipoose Mountains, having to go ahead only a mile or two each day. The road had to be cut and opened for us, and the mountain was covered with snow. With much difficulty we crossed over to the head waters of the Willamette; followed the river down a few days and then gave up the idea of reaching the settlement until spring returned again.

Provisions gave out. Mr. Pringle set off on horseback for the settlements for relief, not knowing how long he would be gone, or whether he could get through at all. In a week or so, our scanty provisions gave out. We were once more in a state of starvation. Much crying and many tears were shed by all but one. She had passed through many trials sufficient to convince her that tears could avail nothing in our extremity. Through all my sufferings in crossing the plains, I had not once sought relief by the shedding of tears, nor thought we should not live to reach the settlements. The same faith and hope that I had ever had in the blessings of Kind Providence strengthened in proportion to the trials I had to encounter. As the only alternative, or last resort, Mr. Pringle's son Clark shot down one of his father's best work oxen and dressed it. We had then something to eat— poor bones to pick without bread or salt.

I must now digress a little. The year of '43, Orus Brown came to Oregon to look at the country. Very likely you saw the publication of Dr. White, Orus Brown, Chapman and one other being taken by the Pawnees in 1845. In '45, he returned. He had three other men with him.

In '46 when we started for Oregon, Orus was appointed pilot, having crossed the plains twice before. His company was six days ahead of ours. He had gone down the old emigrant route and reached the settlements in September. In six or eight weeks, he had heard of the suffering emigrants at the south. He set off with four packhorses and provisions for our relief. He met Mr. Pringle, turned him about, and in a few days they were at our camp.

We had all retired to rest in our tents, hoping to forget our troubles until daylight should remind us of our sad fate. In the gloomy stillness of the night, hoofbeats of horses were heard rushing to our tents. Directly a halloo; it was the well-known voices of Orus Brown and Virgil Pringle. Who can realize the joy? Orus by his persuasive perseverance encouraged us to one more effort to reach the settlement. Five miles from where we were camped, we fell in with a company of half-breed French and Indians with packhorses. We hired six of them and pushed ahead. Again our provisions were becoming short; we were once more on allowance until we reached the first settlers; then our hardest struggles were ended.

On Christmas Day at 2:00 P.M., I entered the house of a Methodist minister, the first I had set foot in for nine months. He requested me to take charge of his house and family through the winter; his wife was as ignorant and useless as a heathen goddess. My services compensated for my own board and Captain Brown's through the winter.

For two or three weeks of my journey down the Willamette,

17

I'd something in the end of my glove finger, which I supposed to be a button. On examination at my new home in Salem, I found it to be a six-and-one-fourth cent piece; this was the whole of my cash capital to commence business in Oregon. With it I purchased three needles; traded off some of my old clothes to the squaws for buckskin, and worked it into gloves for the Oregon ladies and gentlemen. This cleared me upwards of $30 extra of boarding.

Now, my dear relatives, I think you would like to rest awhile. I should like to be present to hear the comments. . . .

TABITHA BROWN

The Brimfield Heroine Letter Continued

Letter 2 page 1

IN MAY '47 I LEFT SALEM, which is now our seat of government, for Oregon City thirty miles down the Willamette in an open boat in company with my Methodist minister and family; from there down the Columbia River to the Pacific Ocean. Here I spent the summer at Clatsop Plains, a settlement south of the bay. At that time there were but ten families residing there. I boarded with a Mr. Pray and lady, missionaries from Ballston, N.Y., a very genteel family; and spent the summer in visiting and bathing in the ocean. The surf of two oceans has rolled over me, Atlantic and Pacific.

In October, I started in an open boat up the river for Salem again, wind and tide against us; was thirteen days reaching Oregon City. Here I was within twenty miles of Tualatin Plains, Orus Brown's location. It would never do for a mother to pass by. Luckily, I found a man with an empty wagon going out, who lived neighbor to Orus. I gave two dollars for my passage, calculating to spend two weeks only with O. and family and reach Salem before the winter rains set in. Went to a Presbyterian meeting on Sunday. After meeting, Orus gave me an introduction to Mr. and Mrs. Clark, missionaries from New York who came here in 1840.

They invited me home with them to spend a few days. Winter set in. They pressed me hard to spend the winter with them. I accepted their invitation. Our intimacy ever since has been more like that of mother and children than strangers. They are about the same age as my own children, and look to me for advice.

My children and the grandchildren who are settled for themselves are all doing well, and are what in the States would be considered wealthy. Orus owns one section of the best of land in the center of this plain, nearly one-half under improvement; a two-story, white frame house; his farm well stocked with horses, cattle, and hogs; and clear of debt.

Pherne's husband has the same five miles from this plain. He has other town property in Salem. His daughter Virgilia married a Mr. Smith from Rochester, N. Y. His two eldest sons Alvin Clark and Andrew Orus are married; all doing well within one hour's ride of him. Alvin . . . I am staying with for a short time. He has one of the handsomest and most valuable half-sections in the country, joining his father, well stocked and well fenced. . . . He is clear of debt and a worthy young man.

Back to my narrative once more. In October, 1847, news from the suffering emigrants told of much sickness and death on the plains, and many poor orphan children left to an unfeeling world to be cared for by strangers. I said to Mr. Clark: "Why has Providence frowned on me and left me poor in this world? Had He blessed me with riches as he has many others, I know right well what I should do."

"What would you do?" was the question.

"I should establish myself in a comfortable house and receive all poor children and be a mother to them."

He fixed his keen eyes upon me and asked if I was candid in what I said.

"Yes, I am."

"If so, I will try with you and see what we can do."

Mr. Clark was to take the agency and try to get assistance to

19

establish a school for the first time in the Plain. I should go into the old log meetinghouse, and receive all the children, rich and poor. Those whose parents were able were to pay $1.00 a week, including board, tuition, washing, and all. I agreed to labor one year for nothing; Mr. Clark and others agreed to assist me so far as they were able in furnishing provisions, provided there was not a sufficiency of cash coming in to sustain the poor. The time fixed upon was March '48.

In April I rode up to Salem to visit my children. Captain Brown died at my granddaughter Smith's while I was there at Mr. Pringle's. I did not see him till after he was dead. He had been delighted with Oregon; became very fleshy; spent his time with people from eastern cities; and felt himself at home. He enjoyed life too well—was too advanced in life to nerve himself for so many exciting attentions bestowed upon him by reason of his age and gentlemanly deportment, whatever company he fell in with. It was a novelty to see a man so old in Oregon. He sank under it, was taken with shortness of breath, and died in an hour. He had joined the Methodist Church there in Salem, as no Presbyterian church was nearer than forty miles.

(NOTE: It may be interjected here that in 1847 when Tabitha left Salem for her stay in Forest Grove, Captain Brown was again his rugged self. Later, Captain Stark of the old Atlantic Coast days had brought his ship in to Portland. He went to Salem to see his old friend and persuaded Uncle John—then in his eightieth year—to accompany him in Stark's ship to San Francisco. There with other friends they had a happy time for several weeks. Uncle John returned very much overweight, with a new supply of memories, a fine outfit of new clothes, and extravagant presents for his relatives, as in the old, young years in New England. We of the present can scarcely comprehend that in pre-railroad days the captain of a clipper ship who had sailed to Far Eastern countries was an unusual person in any community. When living in St. Charles, he had returned to the East once or twice on business.)

20

Again to my journal: The last Saturday night in April, I arrived at the Plains again, and found all things in readiness for me to go into the old meetinghouse and cluck up my chickens the next Monday morning. The neighbors had collected dishes they could part with for the Oregon pioneers to commence housekeeping. A well-educated lady from the East, a missionary's wife, was the teacher. My family increased rapidly. In the summer they put me up a house. I had now thirty boarders of all sexes and ages from four years to twenty-one. I managed them, did almost all my own work but the washing, which was always done by the scholars.

In the spring of '49, we called for trustees; had eight appointed; they voted me the whole charge of the boardinghouse free of rent; established the price of board at $2.00 a week, and what I made over above my expenses was my own. In '51 I had forty in my family, at $2.50 a week. Mixed with my own hands 3,423 pounds of flour in less than five months.

Mr. Clark, for the establishment of the school, gave over to the trustees one-fourth section of land for a town plot. A large building is upon the spot we selected at the first meeting. It has been under town incorporation for two years; and at the last session a charter was granted for a university to be called Pacific University with a limitation of $50,000. The President and Professor are already here from Vermont. The teacher and his wife in the Academy are here from New York.

You must be your own judges whether I have been doing good or evil. I have labored hard for myself and the public and the rising generation. But I now have quit hard work and live at my ease. I am independent as to worldly concerns. I own a very nicely finished white frame house Gothic style, eight rooms on a lot in town within a short distance from the public buildings. That I rent for $100 per year. I have eight other town lots with outbuildings worth $150 each—have eight cows and a number of young cattle. The cows I let out for their milk and one-half the increase. I have rising $1,100 cash due me. Four hundred of it I have donated to the university, besides $100 of it I gave to the Academy three years ago. This much I have ac-

21

cumulated by my own industry and good management independent of my children, since I drew six-and-a-quarter cents from the finger of my glove.

THE BEAUTY OF OREGON

Lower Prices, A Letter

Now I must give you a short description of the beautiful scenery of this delightful and healthful country. The whole of Oregon is delightful, especially the plains, of which there are many. But this West Tualatin is the most beautiful of all others. The outskirts of the Plain are circled around with hills a few miles distant covered to their summits with fine bunch grass, fir, and oak timber. Near the edge the Plain is circled clear around with fir trees green all the year, and standing three-hundred feet high.* In front of them, in contrast with the green, there are large spreading oaks casting their shades over the farmers' white houses, as there are many in full view. Grass is green here all winter, and cattle get their living without being fed. Snow seldom lies on the ground longer than a few days. Large improvements extend out into the Plain in every direction. You may see at all times large bands of cattle, horses, and people passing in every direction morning and evening.

We have a cool, refreshing breeze from the sea. The nights are cool and pleasant. We sleep under almost as much clothing in summer as in winter. I wish you could see this country. We have no prevalent diseases here. Most of the deaths that occur are of emigrants whose systems were diseased before leaving the States. It is very seldom that we hear of a child dying that was born in Oregon.

I do not have time or space to give you the Oregon prices current. Everything in the farming line has been very high, and merchandise very low. But at this time all is low. Horses last

---

* It is noticeable that when Mrs. Brown was writing of the forests in Oregon another native of Massachusetts (born in Concord) was at the same time describing the trees of Walden Pond and his happiness there.

22

spring were valued at from $200 to $300; American cows, $100. I could have taken $800 for my eight cows; now I could not get more than $60 per head.

Adieu for the present,
TABITHA BROWN

George H. Atkinson, D.D., Secretary of the Board, to Mrs. Tabitha Brown

Oregon City
May 15, 1857

DEAR MADAM: I feel grateful for your agency in attending to the matter. . . . In a few days we will be out and settle the whole question in a meeting of the Board, and have the writings passed. I think that you had better have the writings drawn if necessary to hold the parties to the bargain until we come. But if not, the writings can be left until we meet.

If we take the "site" at the limits proposed, it will be in fact a purchase of the land and a payment in the subscription.

Of course the deed must be for a consideration, and the consideration should be six hundred dollars, or eighty or ninety dollars per acre. Mr. Marsh will survey the land outside the fence, and thus by knowing the number of acres, we shall know the rate we pay.

Yours very truly,
G. H. ATKINSON

P.S. You will see that we must compromise by a purchase, instead of yielding a principle. I find that we must go into a suit of chancery to get the original ten acres. Rather than do that, I prefer to purchase as you have provided.

G.H.A.

NOTE: Mrs. Brown also chose the location of the first building, a place with tall oaks.

Excerpts From Virgil Pringle's Diary

WEDNESDAY, APRIL 15, 1846—Left this day with my family for Oregon.

16th—Two families joined us and we went ahead seventeen miles. . . .

20th—Fine road. Went twenty miles. Grand Prairie, Boone County. . . .

27th—Thunder storm. Crossed Crooked River and camped on wet ground.

28th—In Ray County. Roads good. Passed Camden and arrived at Manthano Brown's, having traveled thirteen miles. Broke tongue of the first wagon O. bought, about a hundred yards from Brown's house.

April 29th–May 1st—Remained at Brown's. Put new tongues in wagons and made two new yokes. Employed ourselves at other arrangements for the trip.

May 2nd—Left Manthano Brown's and went about six miles, camping in Missouri bottom about one mile from the ferry.

May 3rd—Came to ferry and found the crossing slow. Occupied the day in getting our wagons across. . . .

7th—Arrived at Independence. Finished our outfit and went four miles. Our teams doing well and not overloaded. . . . Rocks in ledges, springs, trees.

10th—Left the Santa Fe road. Six miles over beautiful prairie. Came into corral with the whole emigration in sight. Divided into two parties.

13th—Traveled twenty miles to the Kansas River. Kaw Indians plenty about. Ferry consists of two flatboats owned by a Shawnee Indian. . . .

17th—Hills parallel with the Kansas. Several oxen overcome

24

with heat. Stopped three hours on a branch. Encamped this night near a Kaw village.

20th—Blue River rising fast. Detained by the water two days.

21st—Crossing the Blue River by fording. Raised our wagons by placing blocks between the beds and bolsters, and went over dry. . . .

25th—The most violent hurricane overtook us. The wind blew from every point of the compass with the utmost violence, but principally from the southwest, and the rain fell in torrents. Its severity was such as to blind a man and take his breath away. It continued about forty-five minutes when it abated.

26th—Examined our wagons and put our clothing to dry. Our provisions generally dry and in good order. A company of thirteen wagons overtook us.

29th—Find the country less rolling and the sand increasing. Arrive at the Blue Earth River and find it up and over the low bottom. Known as the Republican Fork.

30th—Eighteen miles. Some antelope and elk and other game. Grass short but good.

June 2nd—Leave the Blue Earth. Set our course for the Platte. Fifteen miles. Killed the first antelope. Mr. Shelton had a daughter die this night occasioned by scarlet fever before they left the States, having lost another child since they left home.

4th—Went ahead until 12:00 and made preparations to bury the child, which was done in a decent manner, considering the circumstances, in an elevation of the prairie near the head of Grand Island. Camped on the bank of the river which is nothing but a broad vale of sand with banks about three feet high, which are full at high water.

5th—Met Pawnee Indians returning from the north with horses packed with skins.

6th—Pass thirteen boats for St. Louis from Fort Laramie all loaded with peltry and fur. They draw about a foot of water.

8th—Twenty-two miles and camped near the junction of the two forks of Platte.

9th—A great day for hunters. Buffalo and antelope. Water warm and bad tasting. Alkaline efflorescence mixed with salt-peter. Found thirty-three wagons from St. Joseph, having been there a week hunting cattle where a hundred head had strayed away from them.

12th—Crossed the river. Pulling hard through the sand. Put double teams to our wagons. The distance with the angle we took was 1½ miles.

13th—Currants and chokecherries. The country appears to be formed by the wind blowing out sand in basins, some of which are forty feet deep.

18th—Visited Parker's Castle. Saw the "Chimney" some twenty miles distant. (NOTE: Deep-cut wheel tracks in soft marl show where wagons of the Oregon Trail had passed. Nearby rocks have names and initials that have stood the weathering more than a century.) I made twenty miles and camped near Scott's Bluff.

19th—Passed The Chimney in the fore part of the day. Camped near Scott's Bluff.

22nd—A Sioux encampment of about twenty lodges. They were moving on to Fort Laramie where we found about two hundred lodges of Sioux. A disagreeable day with sand filling the air. . . . Camped last night with about seventy wagons. This morning all united in giving our Sioux brethren a feast, with which they appear highly pleased. It was conducted with considerable order and regularity on their part. Smoked the pipe of peace. A friendly address from their chief. A present of powder, lead, and tobacco on our part. This done, we went about six miles and camped on the river.

24th—We deviated from the usual route on leaving the road, which is over highlands between the Platte and Laramie. Ours was up the Platte. Traveled nine miles and intersected the old road at the spring. We now enter the Black Hills. Six miles and camped on the bank of a clear mountain stream.

25th—Find timber plenty on the creek. Cottonwood, box, willow, and ash.

July 1st—Found three trappers at the ford. They had been successful in catching beaver this spring on ground that had not been trapped for fifteen years.

2nd—Left the North Fork and took to the mountains through desert, the first time we have seen land that appeared perfectly sterile.

3rd—Dined at a place of very singular miry wells. Two of our cattle were mired before we discovered them. The wells . . . when I place my foot on them show no more resistance than water. Killed a buffalo after we camped. Near Independence Rock after eighteen miles over hard-pulling sand on the banks of the Sweetwater. In a high region. Frost both this and yesterday morning.

Wind River Mountains. Big Sandy . . . Green River . . . Fort Bridger . . . Bear River. . . . A village of Shoshone Indians, six hundred traveling up the river . . . yellow currants . . . eighteen miles and camp near Soda Springs.

[When they had been on the long journey for several fairly pleasant months, they did not call it roasting meat on the grill in the patio, or a vacation with hunting companions, but perhaps it was partly both; they knew how to broil bison, bake biscuit, and fry cured meat over the glowing coals of a campfire! (And the women had spare time to make drawings and watercolor sketches of scenes they found, or of places they had left behind.)]

August 2nd—Enjoy the novelties of Soda Springs.

3rd—Calamity. . . . Son six years old fell from the wagon and the wheels ran over his head. The remainder of the day occupied in burying him.

4th—Leave Bear River and camp on Portneuf, a branch of the Snake. Seventeen miles.

August 18th—At this place the Oregon and California roads fork. Took the California road, intending to follow it about three hundred miles. . . .

Sept. 6th—Hot Spring Valley . . . to desert of fifty-five miles. . . . Left two steers on the road . . . greasewood and sage . . . teams badly jaded . . . Bad road . . . rocky . . . steep hills down into canyon . . . Klamath Lake country . . . Klamath River. . . . Route continues over spurs of mountains and through thick timber. Great loss of property and suffering. . . . Pheme and the

27

girls obliged to walk. Oxen weak. . . . Lay by to repair shoes and lay in stock of meat. Get three deer and a salmon from the Indians.

November 14th—Bury Mrs. Bounds who died the day before.

19th—Climb another ridge with double teams and make two miles. One steer dies.

23rd and 24th—Move one mile.

25th—Camp on the Willamette River, the handsomest valley I ever saw. All charmed with the prospect.

26th—Lost two steers by the cold.

Monday, November 30—Commence making a canoe for going to the settlement for supplies. Continue until December 3rd. I then start ahead on horseback for beef, leaving the others to finish the canoe and go down the river. I met Orus Brown in company with some others coming with packhorses to bring in those left behind. I returned with them and was from this to the 25th of the month getting my family to Salem, the weather all the time rainy and swales of water to wade every day. Left my wagons and cattle at the forks of the river.

I would conclude this journal by saying that I was well pleased with the society and location of Salem, was kindly received, and such indulgences granted me as I needed.

The complete logbook or diary, the original copy, Pherne's book of sketches, and also some family letters are held by Pacific University.

Virgil Pringle was bringing not only carpenter's tools, but shoemaker's tools and supplies for the upkeep of the family footwear—for his wife, three daughters and two sons. Also, there was a third wagon packed with favorite shrubs and plants for the home in "paradise," as they "would be there in September," and they intended to live well. (We may remember that this was long before the iron horse crossed to Oregon carrying freight.)

The Weather and the Mileage

VIRGIL PRINGLE was not exaggerating about the "swales" of water, and that year they did come before Christmas. "The windows of heaven opened and all the earth was then covered with water," though it was not as deep as in the days of Noah, and it did not dampen the enthusiasm.

As to Mrs. Brown, she may have believed that the uses of adversity are sweet, as in her rhapsody there was no dolorous interlude on the theme of the rainy season.

After seven years in Salt Lake City, one arrives at the conclusion that in the dampish period the beautiful valley of peaches, plums, and prunes (with lombardies and alfalfa) falls in line with the far Northwest for two or three months:

> In winter it rains when folks on the plains
> Are busy shoveling snow;
> When the downpour's o'er life goes as before,
> For spring has come, they know.
> —*This Broad Land*

It may be added that all who can do so flee to some other state in desperation to see a patch of blue. Then, tiring of continuous sunshine, they soon are longing to see a cloud and some miry clay being tracked up onto the pavement!

Mr. Pringle's reference to the "hurricane" was eye-arresting, as this reporter has had experience and some "close calls" with tornadoes. He was then at headquarters for those twisters.

Midwest Tornado

(Nebraska)

The day is fair; the air is clear;
The western sun is riding high.
When now my journey I begin,
There is a blue and cloudless sky.

And then as if from out the earth,
In a near by open level space,
A small white fluffy cloud appears
And offers challenge for a race.

Its upper side with billows white
Reflects the sun in glaring rays,
While through the darkness underneath
The flashing sharp-tongued lightning plays.

This sudden storm in miniature
Drags through a field of ripening grain,
And then from out the blue there comes
A heavy, swift downpour of rain.

But, as my journey leads me on,
I gaze in wonder and surprise,
For all around on every side
The bent and broken wreckage lies.

And here a house is cut in two,
And there a roof is torn away;
Now, many trees uprooted lie
As if strewn out in fiendish play.

And then I see atop a fence
Long blades of grass arranged with care
As if an unseen hand had picked
And sorted out and hung them there.

The people wander 'round about
Where homes were carried far away;
And dazed, they walk the country roads
And view the grain fields in dismay.

When other villages I see,
The same destruction 'round me lies,
As if the fury of the air
The puny work of man defies.

—*This Broad Land*

Strange Parasol

(Wyoming)

I drive along a barren place
On hard and smooth dry clay;
It is an open level space
And the hills seem far away.

Now suddenly an iron pipe tall
Thrust tightly in the ground
Throws out a misty parasol
And spreads it all around.

A thirsty giant is the air—
He drinks the fine white spray;
No tiny brooklet find I here
From the spring to run away.

—*From Mountain to Shore*

Early Names

"Oh, shades of Kit Carson and Bridger," I'd say,
Horace Greeley I might mention, too!
Oh, what would they say in Wyoming today
Of this fine western city I view?
—*From Mountain to Shore*

Two Branches of the Browns in Oregon

PAUSING MOMENTARILY, we recall those early days by the Mississippi when the first wife of Orus Brown, who was a descendant of Increase Mather, passed on, leaving two little sons. The elder, Alvin Clark, was a tiny tot, and Andrew Orus an infant. Tabitha had taken those two little children and cared for them until Orus was married a second time. Subsequently, when the Brown clan was well settled in Oregon, these two grandsons still lived near Tabitha.

But the Pringles all chose Salem as headquarters for their branch of the family tree. This brings to mind a saying we find in German. *Er wird nie auf einen grünen Zweig kommen.* (He will never amount to much.) Yet so far as reported to this recorder, the Pringles were all green and growing satisfactorily along the banks of the Willamette.

Moreover, there was another reason for separating Browns and Pringles. The Episcopal Rector at St. Louis had advised them all to unite with the Methodist Church in Salem, as there was no Episcopal Church in the area. The Pringles did so, but Tabitha Brown did not. She still clung to her Episcopal Prayer Book and Bible for devotional reading and to her husband's sermons (as well as to the miniature of him which showed the plush of the outside cover worn down to the warp).

Therefore, Tabitha's interest was centered in her beloved orphan school under the Congregational Church, while the Pringles at Salem became sponsors of Willamette University, the Methodist College there. It appears that Tabitha went to Salem only as a visitor, except when at the end she spent her last days with Mrs. Pringle.

There was an earlier school nearby for Indians and half-breeds only, with classes meeting in the home of Harvey Clark, the missionary. As stated elsewhere, that Indian school was soon abandoned, and later Mr. Clark moved to Forest Grove where he worked with Mrs. Brown for the orphan school. (This has been well proven from authentic records).

Excitement Over the Oregon Question

THERE WERE SOME who did not welcome the oncoming tide of emigration moving toward Oregon. Besides, they would have left Montana a nearly trackless wilderness while they were occupied in expanding their fur and fish operations along the Columbia.

As to our Brown and Pringle Pilgrims, it was not the much-discussed freedoms that had brought them to Oregon; those they already had and continued to take for granted. It was the lure of another list of "f"s; forest, fur, fish, fertile soil, and favorable climate. This was their "Paradise." They had followed a definite dream. It is surprising to see how soon they had moved from the original log homes into roomy, two-story houses usually with siding painted white against a background of dark green forest.

Now we may note that our Oregon pilgrims probably were never farther north in Dakota than the Black Hills of South Dakota. Little did they or other settlers at that time know of the riches lying near the surface of the famous hill in Butte! We now know that it was not until the last decades of the nineteenth century that Anaconda joined in the "Big Boom" that swept the country—that period when many railroads were being built.

Also, we may observe that in those days of the far-flung territories parts of them were being carved into smaller areas and named as states. We find it was not until 1889 that Montana became a state. It is noticeable that the western part of Montana was taken away from Oregon (which had already become a state in '59).

But that same western part—that area west of the Great Divide—was in several ways tied with Oregon. Even today in crossing the Rockies one is very soon really falling and sliding down the Western Slope.

As Mr. Isaac F. Marcosson in *Anaconda,* his recent volume, comments, "Montana was successively a part of Missouri, Nebraska, Idaho, Dakota, and Oregon Territories."

We may mention here that it had been in 1844, the same year when Orus Brown had stayed over in Oregon, that there were many discussions over the northwest boundary line. The presidential campaign included many heated and stormy scenes before the question was finally settled in '46 (exactly when our Pilgrims were traveling) by compromise with British America. The line was fixed at 49° north latitude.

It appears that in the eastern states the public was very familiar over a long period with the fur operations of John Jacob Astor at Astoria. His trading post at the last point on the Columbia was where the Indians coming down from the far north had landed their boatloads of pelts. It had been claimed that the post was owned by the Hudson Bay Company.

The Oregon settlers were thankful and very much relieved that their country had not been traded for a cod fishery along some frozen shore in the far Northeast.

It was that last point of land around which Tabitha Brown had sailed that first summer and had passed by the rain forest, perhaps on her way to Seaside where "the waves of the Pacific Ocean have rolled over me."

Some thirty years ago it seemed a strange experience to be

34

walking at high tide on boards supported by piling with the breakers rushing through the piling just below one's feet—and that was on the main business street of town. It sounded weird. Then looking across to the Washington shore, the bay seemed five miles wide.

It was along here and on rough water that Tabitha Brown spent thirteen days in an open boat on the return journey!

Let us turn aside to honor the memory of Marcus Whitman who made the long and hazardous journey back to Washington to convince the authorities there that it was highly important to settle that boundary line at once.

What happened? We chatted over the garden fence, said "Good morning" to our neighbors, and agreed that their gulls were welcome to eat our grasshoppers; also, we in return would allow their children to come over and holler down our rain barrel when it was empty, and they were working over their fields of wheat. We did not bother to unpack our boxing gloves, or to brush the moths out of our winter coats. It was as simple as that.

Discovering Unknown Wonders

WHEN NAPOLEON'S AIRCASTLES were taking wings and flying away, he needed some extra pennies—or, rather, *francs*—for loose change (our forebears would have called it "ready money" or sometimes "cash money")—*vielleicht brauchte er schnell ein wenig Trinkgeld für den Kellner. Wahrscheinlich war es nötig.* Anyway, in 1803 he had sold us a dozen or so states across the plains for $15,000,000, stretching to the top of the Great Continental Divide, the line curving eastward with the Arkansas River.

It is still more interesting to remind ourselves that even in those early days of barter and exchange of items we paid cash in plain dollars for that little garden plot.

35

It is well to remember now that President Jefferson had sent Lewis and Clark as early as 1804 to explore the new Northwest. Traveling in river boats, the party went up the Missouri to Bismarck, North Dakota. There they were frozen in for the winter. It is said that Sacajeweah, a young Indian girl, gave them directions and valuable information. With the coming of spring they went on their way upstream and found the source of the Missouri at Three Rivers in Montana.

There they saw the geyser water rushing down from the mountains and named the streams Jefferson, Madison, and Gallatin (three prominent names at the time). The explorers were much gratified to learn how the Missouri River was formed. We may recall that Meriwether Lewis with his pleasing name had been Private Secretary to President Jefferson who planned the expedition.

This leads us directly to the cabinet of President Thomas Jefferson. This includes Albert Gallatin, Congressman, United States Senator, and Secretary of the Treasury, 1801–13. This period included the eight years of Jefferson's administration, and was, of course, of the utmost importance in the story of our country. Gallatin helped us to arrange our peace with England on Christmas Eve, 1814, in the city of Ghent.

In these hurried and harried days, let us pause to sing the praise of Gallatin as Secretary of the Treasury with James Madison, the next President, as Secretary of State. A strong team, indeed! It is well to recall that with rare foresight and understanding during that time in Ghent our Gallatin, instead of arguing over interference with our shipping, settled half a dozen issues in that treaty of 1814, clearing a path for the exploring of our Louisiana Purchase and our rapid growth.

Now this ties in, so to speak, with the story of the Browns, for it was during that same period of unpleasantness in Europe that Captain John Brown's boat, a clipper ship, was sunk by the French as contraband of war. He was rescued, clinging to his water-soaked and ruined logbook, but was held for a time as prisoner.

Also, though it was more than forty years after the Big

Purchase when our Browns and Pringles went west, much of the new area was still a wilderness. It is interesting to notice that some editors in the East had predicted the day when that strange land would actually have towns and cities with busy roads and with river boats carrying goods to the west coast to be shipped to the Orient; they did not predict the iron horse climbing the Divide. Again as to the rivers: We come to a better appreciation of the naming of those streams for our statesmen. This observer has stood by the Missouri's large tributary, the Yellowstone, when the water was high, and where the river is very wide as it goes hurrying down from the famous park and lake. The raging torrent was carrying logs and uprooted green trees that came tossing and rolling to join the Muddy Mo, an impressive scene, indeed. A memory picture shows immense willows calmly drinking water along the river's bank—a contrasting border for the terrifying flood. This stream and the Little Mo, frequently crossed by this recorder at Medora, bring their heavy loads of yellow clay and muddy the whole stream, though the latter may be seen as only a dry creek bed with a tiny trickle of water.

Those courageous explorers passed that way, and it was November of 1905 when they reached the mouth of the Columbia. They supposedly returned by the same route, floating downstream and across to St. Louis with a record of eight thousand miles and more.

As to canoeing in the upper reaches of those three small rivers, it cannot be recommended, for they are making wild plunges through deep canyons and high cliffs better known to the eagle and the mountain goat.

A contrasting epic is that of Ezra Meeker. In 1852, six years after the Browns and Pringles, he calmly and serenely, so to speak, drove his team of oxen to Oregon, bringing along his wife and small child. There were no such tragic happenings as befell many others.

Then after fifty years of living as a farmer in the state of Washington, he created much amusement and attracted attention across the country in 1906 by returning to the city of Washington with an ox team, thus advertising the Oregon Trail Association,

37

which he had founded. This resulted in wide interest in marking historical spots. Various western places were named after him. It may be added that later Meeker also followed the trail by plane and train, retracing in many places the exact route of the pioneers.

In 1930 there were celebrations honoring the birth of Ezra Meeker one hundred years before. These included a replica reproduction of an original wagon train with covered wagons, mules, horses and real buggies; Indians in paint and feathers, with men and women in appropriate garb. These twentieth century pilgrims carried greetings from the Governor of Missouri to the Governor of Oregon. Celebrations were held along the way. Probably the largest of these was at Casper, Wyoming, for a few days about July 4, when large crowds of visitors attended. This reporter has an autographed letter of Ezra Meeker.

The Burro and Ways and Means

SMALLER THAN THE ENGLISH DONKEY in the days of Charles Dickens, and much smaller than the mule of the South or the tough Government pack saddle mules of geodetic survey groups, is our burro. This creature, early introduced from Old Mexico, is amusing, stubborn, patient, and sometimes vicious. Our travelers, lost and wandering into New Spain, probably saw no burros then, but Uncle Clark Brown in Old Santa Fe doubtless did. The sure-footed beast bringing ore down the hazardous mountain trails was, of course, early typical of the Old West, together with the prospector, his "grubstake," pick and shovel. And beware of those heels when the ears are pointing backward!

There are stories of wild horses (escapees) having been captured in later years by the Indians, but it appears that the emigrants depended only on oxen and the eastern horses.

It has been often said that during the Great Emigration the daily distance averaged fifteen miles. We know it ranged from twenty to nil. We may venture to opine that it was *poco a poco ritardando con molto largo*—not *allegro molto con furioso*, but always *decresendo scherzo*. (At least that is meaningful.)

Besides, in emergency, they had the flesh of oxen rather than mules.

As to ways and means of travel, some sources have suggested that the Rockies could have been crossed through Colorado where there was a choice of several passes and original Indian trails. But that was much more difficult with higher altitudes at passes, swift mountain streams to be crossed, too swift for rafts or ferries, and often too deep for fording at the time of high water.

It appears that the main route led up the Platte River, over South Pass, across the Green, and along the Powder and Umatilla to the Columbia. Supposedly, the shortest way was some two thousand miles from Independence to Portland.

Ceremonial Dancing

Now I see a ceremonial—
See some ceremonial dancing
(Dancing not as we now know it)
After hearing strong voice calling,
Calling from a western hillside,
Calling all the clan together—
Seeming words from ancient language.
Now I see the line is forming,
Moving now upon the roadway;
Short and measured are the footsteps,
Slow and dignified the manner.
Custom handed down from fathers,
Custom understood by elders,
Ritual handed down from ancients,

39

Ritual known to few men only.
Woman wearing white cloth headband
With a spray of fresh green willow—
Symbols in impressive setting
In the valley by the hillside
Where the willow drinks from creek bank.
In the quiet Sabbath sunlight
Maiden on a snow-white pony,
Pony with elaborate trappings
Wrought with brilliant-colored beadwork
Done with care in many colors.
Now the sunshine on the beadwork
Sparkles 'round the maiden riding,
Making myriad tiny rainbows.
Unfamiliar rites are over,
Still I know not of their meaning.
Soon the tribesmen leave the marching
And return each to his cabin.
Now the road again is quiet,
Now afar the busy traffic.

—From Mountain to Shore

The Rivulet

(Colorado)

In the middle of the street
In a tiny mountain town
Where the hillsides nearly meet,
Comes "Little River" down.

And gracefully it dances
'Neath bridge and fallen tree,

And singing, gaily prances
As it starts down toward the sea.

By a log house near it passes
Or an old deserted store,
Or ore heaped up in masses,
As its rushing rapids pour

Like a clear eternal fountain
Fed by Alpine banks of snow
From its cradle on the mountain
To the valley down below.
                              —*This Broad Land*

NOTE: The rivulet is the South Arkansas near its source by
Monarch Pass and the famous old Madonna mine. It may be
noted that the river joins the main Arkansas in rushing down
from Tennessee Pass and through the Royal Gorge. This is the
boundary of the Louisiana Purchase, so that residents of the river
towns are stepping across that historic line each time they cross
a bridge (and also each time they cross the Great Divide). We
may note that our Browns crossed into Wyoming and passed just
north of this river area, doubtless following the North Platte.

Watching the World Go By

(Colorado)

I'm driving through an abandoned town.
A house is standing near my way;
Doors, windows, chimneys, taken down
Have left but the shell of a house today.

Just now as I am passing by,
A horse in the dining room looks out—

His head through a window holding high,
He views the landscape all about.

Sometime, somebody built that home
And then looked out with happy eye;
He did not know the day would come
When the horse would watch the world go by.
—*From Mountain to Shore*

Dinner Time

(Colorado)

One day a burro in the shade
Of a large and spreading cottonwood
His dinner of newspaper made
And seemed to think it very good.

I thought he ate the want ads first,
Then chewed the editorial section,
And for more knowledge seemed to thirst—
Page one was then his next selection!

He did not mind the printer's ink,
His spirits good did then abound,
Though he was near the river's brink
With green grass growing all around.
—*From Mountain to Shore*

Mrs. Brown Still Had Problems

WHEN WANDERING IN A WILDERNESS, how little did our Pilgrims know each morning what the day would bring. Many decisions were to be made. So it was after they were established in permanent homes. Mrs. Brown was not only much absorbed with the orphans, but with "the rising generations" and with her own grandchildren gathered about her. Her life again became complex. But she was supremely happy; the clouds that gathered about Mount Hood and then came flying overhead all seemed to show their silver linings.

(It may be observed that even here in this small corner the day may bring surprises from that rising generation: A loving friend aged four may remind us that she likes chocolate bars, and what are the chances for a donation, or how about another cookie, and would it be very soon? As a special inducement should she bring the baby over and let me hold him on my lap? This recorder hastily declined the honor, but promised there would soon be a handout. Bribery? No. It is only recognition to folks who promise to step *only* on the grass and dandelions; partly a pattern of co-operation laid down by Grandma Brown.)

We may here recall that Tabitha Brown had still more problems with some of the older students rooming in her own home. She calls attention to the fact that they all lived happily together, even though she allowed some of them to prepare their own meals in her kitchen, and required them to keep their rooms neat. It appears to this scribner, or scrivener, that there was no arguing with Mrs. Brown, for, as she had said, her word was law with the orphans.

> There is beauty in the simple,
> And sublime in everyday things;
> There is drama all about us,

43

Whether in the lives of elders,
Whether in the lives of children,
Whether in the lower kingdoms.
—From Mountain to Shore

The Umpquah Ferry

(1929)

In Oregon I wheel along;
The day and view are fine.
All seems to be a happy song—
When, pronto, a steep incline.

What do I see before my eyes?
A tiny ferry waiting.
No other path before me lies,
And so there's no debating.

A tiny wood platform I see—
It might be called a raft;
One lone man with a pole to be
The captain of my craft.

The long pole hard is pushing now
Against the round rock bed,
Where the crystal stream will ever flow
By clear snow-water fed.

And now I think how strange a ride
Down in this shady place;
Then a shelf road up the steep hillside
High above the river's race.
—From Mountain to Shore

How Little!

The more we learn, the more we find
There's a long way still to go;
The more we learn, the more we find
How little do we know.
                    —*From Mountain to Shore*

Songs of the Train

The western sun is growing dim
As I watch the fading light.
I'm far above the prairie's rim,
For I'm in the Rockies tonight.

A double-header pulls my train,
I hear the engines puff;
They sing not in a sad refrain,
But more in voices gruff:

"I work and work, I'll pull this train
Up to the Great Divide;,
I've succeeded before, I shall again—
Hear me climb this mountainside."

Ere long there are the echoes within
The snowshed at the top,
Escaping steam, a steady din,
For the train has come to a stop.

Important work is going on,
Each airbrake must be tested;
I hear the tapping hammers soon,
Quick voices, a tool requested.

I like the slow and steady start,
And now the brakes are grinding;
The engineer will do his part,
His job he will be minding.

And next I hear the engines say:
"Just list to our steam exhaust,
For we breathe our sighs of relief this way
To think the pass we've crossed.

"But we hold back this heavy train
When the track runs most straight down;
Those brakes grind hard, but do not complain,
Till we reach the roundhouse town."

By daylight now these scenes but serve
To remind of days of yore
As I round each old familiar curve
And hear the river's roar.

By the Eagle River I came down,
And now the Colorado. . . .
As I speed on to each peachtree town
Where many found Eldorado.

In alarm our whistle blows quick blast,
And our speed does somewhat slack,
For a herd of cattle must move fast
To clear the railroad track.

One engine pulls my train today
And seldom does he puff;

46

Meandering around Arroyo's way,
One iron horse is enough.

Now soon we approach the River Green,
Where a fringe of verdure grows,
Contrasting with the surrounding scene
Far below perpetual snows.

Now still I hear the song of the rail
As we cross hard sun-baked clay;
'Twill not be long until we hail
The Wasatch Range today.

Again two horses draw my train,
I hear them huff and puff.
Through Castle Gate I go again;
One steed is not enough.

Through farming towns the whistles blast
'Mid the answering crossing gongs;
And as we reach the city at last,
It's the end of this train's songs.

The Changing Times

THE IRON HORSE now placed in museums has become an antique before our eyes, although in 1900 it seemed the last word; and in the previous quarter-century we know it had really built the West, opening mines and forests. The little adventure described above over Tennessee Pass to Salt Lake City, repeated perhaps a dozen times, is still fresh in mind.

Just before 1800 and a few years afterward certain customs were transposed to another key. Take for example the "given" names among the *hoi polloi* and *bourgeoisie*. Since ancient days

47

a person had borne one label only. Yet for identification sometimes a little geography was added: Saul of Tarsus or Joseph of Arimathea; Jones of the Hill or Smith of the Parsonage.

Later, parents began cautiously giving a child the second or middle name. Let us consider the list of our Presidents: One given name was the rule until the time of Ulysses S. Grant; then came many middle names.

This is also true in the records of Clark and Tabitha Brown. Their only daughter Pherne Tabitha Brown (born 1805) married Virgil Kellogg Pringle—the first appearance of three-part names on the family tree. But, presto, nearly everyone soon had the same!

Some smiles are provided by the old-time picture of all our Presidents as arranged in an oval and mounted in a large walnut frame, showing the evolution of the beard and haircut! Long beards, short beards, pointed beards, round beards, goatees, or clean-shaven chins with heavy, "handlebar" mustaches. And did those honored ones need haircuts? Yes. And so, also, did Poor Richard and others.

Again as to the forebears, we see both Clark and Tabitha using certain words and spellings that have since been changed. They wrote such words as public, pacific, soporific with the final *k*, but sometimes without it. In order to leave the printer blameless, it seems better to delete that *k* entirely. Moreover, both of them sometimes wrote the long *s* in the middle of a word, as in the Gothic script *(deutsche Handschrift)*; this was perhaps related to the long *s* in the middle of a printed word appearing much like an *f*, and very confusing.

Besides, they used "pious" where we would probably choose "religious" or "spiritually minded." The first does sometimes seem to imply insincerity.

Then, too, they used no breathtaking superlatives over small matters, but held in reserve some adjectives for important things, though such were used sparingly.

Now all of this brings to mind that a well-known magazine printed on the front cover the entire twenty-third Psalm in the real Early English. Of course, some words could be guessed, but most of us needed a dictionary of Old English. Do we comprehend the evolution of our language when words banned as slang are now often received in polite society? Or even the coining and borrowing of new words in the last sixty years? Chassis, fuselage, garage, chauffeur did not concern us a few decades ago. And did we feel safe in the trolley or cable cars? We did.

As to Clark and Tabitha, poor mortals, they never had the pleasure of calling a conference a "workshop." Probably they never heard in a classroom, "What is your reaction?" They could have been *dankbar* (thankful). . . . Couldn't it sometimes be idea, impression, inference, understanding, conclusion, or wondering? . . .

Those Browns should have breathed a *"Gott sei dank"* when no commercials came riding the air waves into their homes! They did not have to listen to "toothpaste" in the middle of worldwide news or to a dissertation on onion or garlic in a "tossed" salad. We doubt if Mrs. Brown ever "tossed" salad about the house. We may suppose she had some homemade dill pickles stored away in a keg, and some kraut with "an apple a day" for her orphans. We know her housekeeping was not done by pushing buttons and turning switches. She never heard of orlon or dacron and did not have to decide if she should or would try to navigate on four-inch heels on Sunday morning. Doubtless, she lost no sleep over the latest imported idea of some fashion dictator across the sea. Our pioneers were far more concerned with questions of survival. And it is doubtful if a friend ever telephoned it would be a four-handkerchief film tonight, but last week's picture required only two hankies.

If one change is more impressive than any other, it may be this: the altered attitude toward the books of Jules Verne. This observer recalls being fascinated, as a young girl, by Father's copy of *The Mysterious Island,* published in 1870, and the idea of traveling under water. The public usually scoffed at his writings. A relative was heard saying, "Stuff and nonsense; such things never did happen and never could."

Those prophetic books! His dreams came true in the rapid transport before our astonished eyes.

Now all of this leads us to the conclusion that biography plus biography equals history.

Bryant's Tribute to Mrs. Hemans

*(Her "Forest Sanctuary" was published in 1827
in the old Worcester Talisman)*

THERE IS UNIVERSAL ACKNOWLEDGMENT of her lofty imagination, the depth and clearness of her thought, and her surprising facility in embodying her conceptions. Her lightest efforts thrown off to comply with the solicitations of editors and manufacturers of souvenirs are familiar to every reader. They are seized upon greedily by every newspaper and read and studied and measured in the heart as are the verses of no other man or woman now living.

Mrs. Hemans is the only writer whose words are upon the tongue of every reader, *be he the super of ship news, of bales of cotton, or quintals of codfish. In her longer poems her glory beams forth . . . offerings meet for the acceptance of Apollo. . . .* She accomplishes everything she attempts *by her intimate acquaintance of the human mind. To the honor of the age which may justly boast of its Hemans, she could with safety say,* we believe, that she has never written one line which, dying, she could wish to blot.

When Bryant contributed the above lines, Mrs. Brown was in St. Louis or St. Charles (1824-46). It is probable she was familiar with both Mrs. Hemans and *The Talisman,* especially as women of her day were seldom in public work before the time of suffrage and "women's rights."

50

A Few Facts Condensed

'40—Reverend Harvey Clark came to Oregon.

'40—by Robertson (June, 1905), Oregon Historical Society Quarterly. "Origin of Pacific University" by James Rood Robertson, a careful, scholarly history professor.

FACTS: Harvey Clark, philanthropist, came to Oregon in 1840 as an independent missionary. In the early 40's he had—by holding classes in his home—a school for Indians and half-breeds. That location was about ten miles northeast of Forest Grove. *There was no connection whatever between the two schools.*

By 1844 Mr. Clark had abandoned the school for Indians. In the same year he organized the first Congregational church in Oregon at Oregon City.

In '45 Clark came to West Tualatin Plains (now Forest Grove). There he bought from Orus Brown for five hundred bushels of wheat the claim that Orus had staked out in '43, which included the south part of what is now the Pacific University campus. There in '45 Clark built the second Congregational church in Oregon, having already built the first one for Oregon in Oregon City. At that time there was a thick grove of large fir trees north of where the present Congregational Church of Forest Grove now stands. Clark and Brown spent the whole spring and the early summer cutting trees from that grove and dressing logs and hauling them for the meetinghouse on what is now the college campus. We note that this first meetinghouse was the same building in which Tabitha Brown began her school for orphan children. After Brown had left for the States, Clark and neighbor A. T. Smith with help succeeded in completing this meetinghouse.

Obviously, it was not until late '47 or early '48 that Tabitha suggested having the school. Then Mr. Clark heartily agreed and assisted in many ways.

From Mr. and Mrs. Chester Moffatt
and Daughter Mary

Claridon, Ohio
Oct. 16, 1854

DEAR SISTER:

We have just received your letter with unbounded pleasure. It was read with surprise and wonder how you ever lived to perform such a task, especially for so great a length of time. As you wrote, it must be that God was with you and sustained you. We always find that He is at all times ready to help those that put their trust in Him. . . .

Margaret and I enjoy the blessings of health, but old age has its effects, we think.

C. MOFFATT

DEAR SISTER:

I now for the first time in several years take a pen to add something which the rest have left untold—your kind inquiry after my father's family. . . .

MARGARET MOFFATT

Oct. 18, 1854

DEAR AUNT:

You can picture in your mind's eye your brother's family circle gathered for the evening when your kind, interesting letter was handed in, with what eager anxiety it was perused. Sometimes we were almost afraid to read one more line. Had it come

52

from any other hand than your own, we should have feared to read, but knowing the result gave us courage.

If you could have looked in upon us that night, you would have seen but few dry eyes, your dear brother and sister listening with tears running down their cheeks. It seemed they could not have it so; they could not be reconciled to it that you had passed through such dreadful scenes. "Oh," they said, "how could we have gone to our plentiful table to eat, or retired to rest at night had we known our dear sister was a wanderer among the Rocky Mountains without food or shelter, homeless and alone, yes, worse than alone." How could you think of undertaking the journey? The Eye that never slumbers or sleeps was upon you. . . . Father thinks he shall let it be printed (in Cleveland). It is written in very handsome style and language, and needs but little correction. We have taken much pride in showing it to our friends.

I will give you all the information in my power respecting my father's family: Uncle Lewis . . . Uncle Willis . . . Uncle Joseph, Jr.

MARY MOFFATT

Letters From Harmon and Sanford

Clackamas Ferry
June 11, 1853

MY DEAR MRS. BROWN:

I am putting you up a half barrel of salmon caught by myself. I would that I could present each of my friends at the Grove with one. . . . I now have orders on hand for 100 barrels at $30 per barrel. . . .

I am respectfully,
T. S. HARMON

53

Bowdoin Street, Cambridge
January 3, 1855

MY DEAR KIND FRIEND:

You will see by the above address that I am once more at home. . . . Scarcely a city has improved more in six years than Boston. I have always thought Cambridge one of the pleasantest suburban towns.

I left Portland November 22, crossed the bar in a gale of wind, and landed in San Francisco the 25th. Left Dec. 1 on P.M.S.S. "Sonora," landed at Panama the 17th, and landed at New York the 26th, express train to Boston. Found my family in the Christmas festivities. Our house is about midway between Mount Auburn and Harvard.

I made arrangements to call upon my old pastor. Mr. Beecher, at whose house Henry Ward Beecher is now stopping. He has corresponded with me and now sends an invitation for me to call. Now, "Grandma," will you not give me a few words of remembrance that I may cherish for your sake?

God bless and preserve you. Consider me yours ever to command.

THOS. S. HARMON

San Francisco
August 31, 1857

MRS. BROWN
HONORED MADAM:

You may think strange of receiving a letter from a comparative stranger, but you may remember that I left two daguerreotypes, one of my wife and one of my child, which I should very much like for you to send me if you please. . . .

Since 1851 I have been a wanderer on the globe: I have visited Europe, Asia, and Africa, and also North and South America, and have recovered my health. But I yet feel that I am a homeless wanderer on the face of the earth and no change can shake that feeling from me; but I will not detain you. I am living in San Francisco, but still have that feeling of utter loneliness.

Will you please send me a note and give me the health and prosperity of those I once felt so happy to meet at your house.

Respectfully yours,

G. W. SANFORD

Mrs. Brown in a Lighter Vein

To Her Granddaughter Mary Brown from Tabitha Brown

DEAR MARY:

You are a good girl for writing to me. Oregon abounds in rich bachelors, and I presume, were you here, you might make a tremendously profitable speculation. There are so many ladies coming here by land and by sea that the bachelors have only to watch. . . . You see, they do not like to travel back two or three thousand miles when it can be avoided. I will insure you a profitable trip, and will give you proof to confirm what I say. . . .

I have no more cause to labor for comfort or gain. I have accumulated property more than sufficient for the balance of my pilgrimage here. . . . Tell your father I have all the leisure time I could ask to read and write and prepare for a better world. You are all included in my private devotions. . . .

You would be surprised at the enterprise of the people in ' establishing schools and seminaries through the Territory. Pacific University. . . . I have subscribed $500 to the new building and if the sum comes out lacking, I expect to add $1,000 more. . . .

(The rest of the original letter was lost.)

In another place, Tabitha wrote that she was having a second house built to "rent out" a Swiss style house with eight rooms and two porches . . . and that was in an age when women were not supposed to be in business! Nor were they employed in offices.

55

Tabitha Brown to Her Brother
Chester Moffatt

West Tualatin Plain
December 31, 1854

DEAR BROTHER, SISTER, AND RELATIVES:

Separated as I am from those who were and are dear to me
. . . absent in the flesh . . . been with you in imagination. . . .
*Oh, that it were possible for me to fly, like Peter Parley in
his dream, across the Rocky Mountains!* I have a mind, constitution, and money sufficient for the undertaking, but the hazard
of steamboats and railroads would be my only dread, not that I
have lost confidence in an overruling Providence after so many
proofs of His care over me.

If I could by visiting the States do anything toward advancing
Christ's kingdom in Oregon, I would soon steam for New York
City. Our President and Board of the University are anxious
that I should try the undertaking; they say I could do more and
have a greater influence on the rich nabobs and charitable Chris-
tian people in the cities than any of the trustees here.

The idea of a lady seventy-four years of age coming from the
Pacific coast on a mission from Oregon for the sake of obtaining
funds . . . for the institution which has sprung up by her being
the first to make the proposition; and with Reverend Harvey
Clark giving one-fourth section of land for a town plot! I have
the honor of planting the taproot. . . .

All these things ought to penetrate the hearts of those whom
God has blessed with riches to give bountifully. It is not impossible that I may try the trip yet.

Do not think me vain or boasting by writing what Mrs.
Brown has done and is endeavoring to do in Oregon. President

56

Marsh wishes me to give him the privilege of writing a history of my life, and dividing the profits betwixt me and the institution. I have not agreed to it, nor do I think I have the vanity to comply. . . . I boast not. God had a work for me to do, and had seen fit to use me to accomplish His own purposes. . . . I am but the instrument in His hands.

I am not writing to strangers for notoriety; I am writing to those who were acquainted with me in early life, and to those of equal interest. I am the only aunt of my brother's children. Writing is talking at a distance. I hope you all will view it so. I intend contracting with the editor of the *Oregonian* for the coming year and having him forward it to you at Claridon, Ohio.

Mary, my good niece, I would comply with your request for more details of my adventures, but I am not in the habit of copying my letters—they are all off-hand; so it is more than likely that I would write many events again. Then you would all have to cry for naught, which would be a pity.

I have many details in store from my own experience in life. My early prospects, Mary, were bright and promising but, like the rolling tide, they have been ever ebbing and flowing; sometimes in affluence; at others in penury and want; many have been the hairbreadths I have run since the death of your Uncle Brown. The prosperity and adversity of my life have been, no doubt, intended for my future happiness; we must first be made sensible of the vanities of this world.

I have not occasion to trouble myself about this world's goods; I have sufficient for all my comforts, be my stay long or short. I have quit housekeeping and board out, live at ease, come and go as I please; and as I always have done all my life, I carry my home with me; therefore, I am a stranger to homesickness.

If all in Missouri are living, I have nine grandchildren in Manthano's family, fourteen in Orus', and six in Pherne's—twenty-nine grandchildren and seven great-grandchildren. I have been in most of the States, and find Oregon more prolific than any of them. If there are any in your vicinity who are anxious to become fathers and mothers, send them to the shores of the Pacific.

Say to my nephew Julius that his great little aunt would be delighted to see him in Oregon, but by no means to cross the Plains; be sure to come by the Isthmus.

This much, I think, will do for the present. (With the signature of . . .)

TABITHA BROWN

More Letters to the Moffatts

West Tualatin Plains, O.T.
April 24, 1855

DEAR BROTHER, SISTER, AND FAMILY:

With heartfelt pleasure and satisfaction I received yours of the fifth of March, only one month and six days after date; this much for the invention of steamboats and cars. . . .

I fear I have been too hasty in raising your ideas of a visit from me. Since I last wrote, times have very much changed in New York City.

I am under the impression that Providence has blessed Oregon beyond any other state. . . . We have but little sickness, no drouths, and but two little snow storms during this winter. Peach trees were unthoughtful and bloomed out full in the middle of March. . . . Strawberries are beginning to turn red. . . . I suppose the little streams in Ohio are beginning to ripple on the hillsides from the melting snow above, and the frogs have hardly dared to rise to welcome the return of spring. Not so in Oregon; the earth has been carpeted all winter with green and flowers of every hue and color rise above, dancing in the breeze and glittering in the sunshine.

After giving up crossing the Isthmus last season, I contracted with a carpenter to put me up a Swiss style house with eight rooms on one of my town lots. This has taken nearly all my surplus money. The papers from the States were so filled with distressing accounts by land and by sea where hundreds were swept from the world in a moment. . . . I concluded to build another house to rent, and we must wait a little until I can make another raise. So I commenced housekeeping again.

Do not believe from what I have written that I have given up my trip to Ohio. I only commenced housekeeping for the accommodation of others. There were young ladies wishing to attend school at the Academy, and no one willing to open a boardinghouse. I do not intend to continue any longer than until someone is willing to take my place. By that time I may dispose of some of my town property, and collect some of my out-dues. . . . Did you forward the paper with the extract of my letter in it? if not, please do send me one. . . . I would like to see it. You mention a letter written by brother Joseph's grandson and published in one of the three papers sent. . . . Is he in California? I would like to know if there are any branches of the Moffatt family this side of the Rocky Mountains except my own children.

It will be vacation here the last week in May. Then I intend going up to Salem to see what those Moffatts' *turned Brown* are doing. I wish it were as easy to visit you as it is to go fifty miles to Salem.

Dear brother and sister, this is a beautiful world apart from the people that are in it. How good God must be to bestow such a delightful world with all its treasures on ungrateful man. When I think of my own ingratitude, I am astonished that He has borne with me so long. . . . His benign influence has ever kept me buoyant and happy. If He will only grant me grace . . . for the time to come . . . is my last prayer. May it be yours also.

TABITHA BROWN

Forest Grove
August 30, 1855

MY DEAR MARY:

Yesterday I had the pleasure of receiving yours of the third. My disappointment is equally as great as yours. It has been impossible for me to dispose of property. Besides, there is no one willing to accommodate the students in the way I do, which if I were to quit, would make a vast difference in the number of students. . . . I receive young ladies and a few boys from ten to fifteen years; each furnishes a sufficiency of provisions, bedding, dishes, etc. The girls do the work of whatever pertains to housekeeping under my direction. I am at no expense except for firewood. I have only to give them to understand my law and see that they do not break it.

I never have had occasion to scold or whip any of them. I only say my word is *law,* and all is as it should be. Most of them are strangers to me and to each other, yet a happier set you never saw. There is no discord or contention among them. . . . People here are astonished at the good order and management of my undertaking and say that no one but Mrs. Brown could do the like.

How can I break this chain of usefulness to the rising generation in Oregon, one that all the energy of soul and body has striven to accomplish ever since I first came into this Plain?

Continue to write as usual if you love

AUNT TABITHA BROWN

West Tualatin Plain
Washington County, Oregon T.
January, 1856

DEAR MARY AND ALL INTERESTED PERSONS:

. . . Undoubtedly, you have ere this the information of the excitement here in your Oregon paper.

At first there was a general alarm and the whole country was in an uproar until the proper measures were taken. For the first few days and nights the people lay down to rest with their clothes on. . . . The times were scary and the nights dismal. I would try to make myself as comfortable as I could. At present we have no reason to fear on the Willamette.

I suffered far more in the excitement than when along on the spur of the mountains. Then there was but Captain Brown to suffer with me . . . but now there were not only my children,

Tabitha Moffatt Brown (Mrs.
Clark Brown), May 1780—May
1858.

Clark Brown as a young man in
New England. For many years a
Congregational minister, he had
changed to the Episcopal de-
nomination shortly before his
untimely death in 1817.

Virgil K. Pringle, called "a young Vermonter," but said to have been born in Connecticut.

Mrs. Virgil Pringle (Pherne Tabitha Brown), only daughter to Clark and Tabitha Brown, born in Montpelier, Vermont.

The three daughters of Virgil and Pherne Pringle: (*l. to r.*) Emma Pringle Hughes, Sarelia Pringle Northup, Virgilia Pringle Smith. Another daughter, Mary Ella Young, was born in Oregon. All lived in Salem, except for the Northups, whose residence was in California. It is said that their son, Octa Manthano, was the engineer and director of the first public irrigation canal in eastern Oregon, opening up a large area for irrigation previously supposed to be useless, except for grazing sheep.

Two small flower prints from Mrs. Pherne Brown Pringle's book of sketches made when crossing the plains in 1846.

The prickly pear and a cactus with dark-red blossoms, and low-growing yucca are found by the banks of the Arkansas where irrigation could have been used. This scene is such as the Browns sometimes passed when without water or grass.

Mining camp in the Rockies.

Glimpse of road through prairie grass. These wheel tracks on hard-ba clay, with frequent turnouts, were found on main transcontinental r between stretches of gravel top before 1930. They often ran paralle the railroad.

he Brown-Pringle party, lost and wandering in California, doubtless saw the
dwoods.

Letter from Tabitha Brown to her grandchildren. This sample shows her fine firm handwriting even during her last years.

divided between my three children, & Mrs ___
___ To prevent hard feelings amongst my
children, I have appointed Mr Marsh my
executor — If the mare at Mr Platts should
have a colt as soon as she is old enough to wean
I wish you to attend to it — I give it to Eddie for
his riding horse — — I have recovered from
my last attack and shall calculate if my life
is spaired, to be at the Grove when the traveling
becomes good — Give my love to your Father,
and all that have a sprinkling of my blood,
and say to them — I wish, and pray, them all
to seek to be Christians if they wish to be happy
in this, & the world to come — Virgil is hurrying
& I can write no more —

                                    P. Brown

Sarah and E. Smith,
        I sympathise with you Sarah in the
loss of your Dear Mother —

Evan I have forwarded your Grandpa letters to
        your aunt Sarah as I rec'd it from his exchange
Mary says kiss the Children for her — of Sermons —

A high mountain fastness showing a miniature canyon cut in rock by a tiny stream known as North Fork. It soon pours into "The Rivulet," known locally as Little River—the South Arkansas.

Falls of North Fork at end of canyon, not far from Monarch Pass, the highway following an ancient trail. Little River, the South Arkansas, after being joined by North Fork and two other creeks, empties into Big River; then makes a wild rush through the canyon of the Arkansas and roars through the Royal Gorge.

The lavender-and-white columbine, state flower of Colorado, has its habitat up near the 11,000-foot timberline. These showy blossoms flourish in open sunny spaces amid unbelievably barren fields of boulders.

This building of Pacific University (now the Museum) was the realization of the hopes and dreams of Tabitha Brown. She gave sizable sums of cash as well as real estate and the last ten years of her life to her beloved school. We note the long panels of glass at both sides of front door and by an upper window (reminding one of old-time architecture) as well as the cupola, similar to that of Mount Vernon, beneath which the Browns had slept for several weeks in 1815.

Two buildings on campus of Pacific University.

Lower picture shows one of the early buildings.

This marker, the gift of an ea[r] class in the college, shows t[he] place of Mrs. Brown's first orph[an] school in the old log meeti[ng] house. A tourist stands by t[he] petrified stump to show its re[la]tive height.

The Tabitha Brown Tree on the campus is shown after the top had been taken off by lightning. (See horizontal line at top.) It was later known also as The Old Bee Tree after a swarm of bees had moved into the hollow trunk. An adult stands by to show the height of the tree.

Mrs. Pherne Brown Pringle, nearly 86, is seen enjoying a winter day at her home in Salem, Oregon. With her is a grandson, Clifton Young. This home is where Tabitha Brown spent her last days after retiring from her school. The Pringles had "kept house" for Captain Brown in his home when they were first married.

Bouquet for a last farewell. One of a collection of Pherne Brown Pringle's paintings and drawings that she had framed and hung along the walls in her own room.

Most of the photographs reproduced in this section were supplied by the Tiffany Camera Shop, Marquette, Michigan.

but all the others, especially the women and children collected at my house. But all our fears were of short duration.

God in His wisdom will, I make no doubt, order all things for good. Spring is fast approaching. May the blessings of heaven continue with us through life and at the hour of our death.

TABITHA BROWN

West Tualatin Plain
June 8, 1856

DEAR MARY:

I love you for being so faithful in writing to me. . . .

There was a time to try men's souls, dark days and nights to be sure. There was but little eating or sleeping for a number of days. The height of our fears was soon over.

Most of the Indians were taken to a reserve, a tract of land about twenty miles from here. They are supported by the government and are to be taught the arts of civilization by men employed for that purpose. There are nearly two thousand men, women, and children already on the Reserve. The Agent is constantly gathering in all that are willing. Soon there will be a rush for Oregon, and enterprises will go ahead once more. Already a change for the better is perceptible.

This is a great fruit country. You would be surprised to see little switches not more than four or five feet high so loaded with fruit that limbs have to be propped when the fruit is no more than half grown.

How delighted I should be, dear niece, if you were near so we might enjoy each other's society. There is great disparity of age between us yet, notwithstanding my advanced age, I still retain the lively habits of youth. I am thankful that I was blessed with a cheerful disposition, for I heartily believe that it has a tendency to prolong one's life; whereas a gloomy desponding being will cut short the thread of life.

My love to my dear brother and sister. In imagination I see them; almost hear them speak.

TABITHA BROWN

61

MY DEAR BROTHER, SISTER, AND NIECE MARY:

I am busily engaged in preparing to leave tomorrow for Tillamook Bay on the coast, south of the Columbia River. . . . We shall start from here in a wagon and travel forty miles to the Indian Reservation; thence forty miles more on horseback (NOTE: Mrs. Brown was then more than seventy-seven years of age—born in 1780, May 1) on a trail across the Coast Range to the Pacific Ocean. We calculate to travel eight or ten miles a day and camp out.

I am sorry you anticipate so much fear from our Indian neighbors. Thus far we have had no trouble with them this season. In full faith in the protecting hand of Providence, I am once more preparing to camp out in the wilds of an Indian country. If I had the least fear of danger, I should not undertake it.

Love to all who have a sprinkling of the blood of

TABITHA BROWN

Writing from Forest Grove on December 19, 1856, Tabitha, after receiving a newsy letter from the banks of the Mississippi, was passing along some personal items to the Pringle group at Salem. Among these was mention of Warren Pringle going to St. Louis. With her usual little touch of humor, she had begun her letter: "To whom it may concern."

Then returning to the Oregon scene, she informed them that her grandson Matthew Brown had recently married "his Mary Ann," and that they had settled "across the creek" from her in Forest Grove. She expressed the hope that they would always be as happy as when they began housekeeping.

She then sent this message to her granddaughter Mrs. Pherne Brown Bain Strong: "Tell P. I wrote her father's family of Matth's marriage." (NOTE: The father referred to was Manthano Brown, son of Tabitha, who did not go to Oregon.) With her school in mind she continued, "Tell Ella and Natty they must send me some more of their drawings. They are so nice I intend putting them in the Museum.

As usual, my love to all. Tell Virgilia and the girls I intend making a visit in Salem if I live till spring. Adieu—

T. BROWN

It may be added that she had written at the top of the page: We are all well, I believe, and full of business. I know that I am.

Tabitha Brown's Last Letter to the Moffatts

Salem,
Jan. 25, 1858

MY DEAR MARY:*

Since I received your last letter last August, I have been unable to procure my miniature on account of ill health and no artist nearer than twenty-five miles.

In August, I dismissed my boarders and quit housekeeping and gave my house and lot as an endowment to the university. I then took a trip up the Willamette valley and was absent from the Grove three or four weeks. Soon after my return, I was taken too unwell to go to Portland to fulfill my promise to your parents. . . . Father Time is no respecter of persons; he is busily engaged in drawing furrows and disfiguring our faces to convince me that we are but mortal. Our next change will be from mortality to immortality. Oh, that we may all be prepared for this great and last change!

I have enclosed a few lily seeds, the natural, wild production of Oregon. By placing them under your window, the bloom will perfume the whole room; they are very fragrant.

---

* She was writing to both Mary Moffatt and Mary Brown.

I wish your father would send the Lawton blackberry, if it be but one little root. There is not a high blackberry in Oregon, but a great abundance of low, running ones.

I am independent, my brother, as to my future support; the institution is in a prosperous state; the town is growing rapidly; everything appears onward and upward. I expect to return to the Grove in the spring and spend part of my time there and part of it here with my friends and children.

May Heaven's blessings rest on you all. Adieu until you receive another letter from your far-off

AUNT TABITHA BROWN

Tell your mother I now weigh ninety pounds; I formerly weighed ninety-six.

From President Marsh to Tabitha Brown

NOTE: Sidney Marsh, D.D., was the first president of Pacific University. His father was president of the University of Vermont, and his grandfather was the first president of Dartmouth.

The Grove
March 3, 1858

MRS. BROWN
DEAR GRANDMA:

The duty that you have imposed upon me as executor of your will I shall certainly try to perform—for your sake—as faithfully as I can. May it be long before that duty needs performance.

I thank you for your confidence, and again for all your many expressions of kindness and the sympathy that, of howsoever little value it may have been to you, more than anything else kept me from being entirely dispirited. The kindness of your advice and the sincere interest that you have taken not only in the Institution, but in my own affairs, I shall remember with emotion so long as I live.

I rejoice at the calmness with which you are enabled to look forward to whatever a Merciful Providence has in store, and pray that He may sustain you and fit you fully for all His dispensations.

I wish I could see you, but I am employed mentally and physically to the full extent of my power, and certainly cannot get away from my school.

Very sincerely yours,
S. H. MARSH

P.S. Since writing the above, Mr. Porter called to ask if I was expecting any money of you—that you had written to him to pay me $300. He seemed to suppose it was to be paid to me as executor. As in your letter you made no reference to my request to borrow money, I presumed him to be correct. If you intend to lend anything to me, please send me an order on Mr. Porter, if it is from him that I shall receive it. . . . All my plans for building depend now on my success in borrowing something somewhere.

Mr. Clark is very low and, as we all think, cannot hold out very long.

Yours,
S. H. M.

From Tabitha Brown to Robert Porter

Pleasant Hill,
Jan. 29, 1858

MR. PORTER:

I received yours by Monday's mail, and hasten to answer it. You surely know that I place implicit confidence in you to transact business for me at the Grove. I am willing to sell the house and the two lots to Mr. More, provided you think it best, yet I think if the two lots are included it ought to fetch $1,000, but not less than $900. You may sell for nine if you can get no more—the southeast lot included—if Mr. More does not purchase as stated.

If Mr. Kinney will give one hundred sheep (ewe sheep after shearing) and $300 in cash for the other house and lot it stands on, he may have it. I consider your judgment better than my own, so I leave it with you to do as you'd for Robert Porter.

Mr. Pringle says—and so do I—make out your check against Mrs. Bailey and send it here for collection. You can get it at a word, as others have done. She lives in town and has cash aplenty.

My love to Caroline, and tell Ebby and Mary that when Grandma comes, she will fetch them something. How is it with my namesake? Is she as quiet as ever, or is she still "practicing music"?

My health is becoming very good. . . . Virgil and Pherne are determined to use every possible means to restore my health. They will not suffer the least exposure, even to set my foot upon the cold ground. . . . I have been outside the house but once—that was to a dining party at Mr. Smith's. I was invited to spend Christmas at Mr. Minto's, but thought it not prudent to go. We have ten or twelve visits on our list in readiness for pleasant weather. . . .

Give my love to the rest of the family that have any of the same to give in exchange to

T. BROWN

We find her, instead of planning for herself, raising funds for a fine cemetery monument, busily writing of her family, and sending "your Grandpa's likeness" to her eldest grandson. This after she had had several sinking spells.

The following is the last word we have from Tabitha Brown.

Tabitha Brown to Alvin Clark Brown, Her Grandson

Feb. 24, 1858
Salem

MY DEAR GRANDCHILDREN:

I have had another severe attack—different from any of my former ones. I was taken on Friday last, directly after breakfast, with a complete sinking of my whole system, which caused great alarm—so much so that a lawyer was called from town for me to sign the deed to Mr. Mosie, and to write my will. At evening I had recovered sufficiently to write my name.

For fear that you may not have a correct statement from others written to, and as Mr. Pringle is going to start for town in a few moments, I can only write sufficient to let you know that I have donated to five children $100 each and the same amount in reserve for little Edda Brown.

When my bequeath and what is to be paid out of my estate is settled, the remainder is to be divided between my three children: O, Manth., P———. To prevent hard feelings amongst my children, I have appointed Mr. Marsh my executor.

If the mare at Mr. Flett's should have a colt, as soon as it is old enough to wean, I wish you to attend to it. I give it to Edda for his riding horse.

I have recovered from my last attack and shall calculate, if my life is spared, to be at the Grove when the traveling becomes good.

Give my love to your father and all that have a sprinkling of my blood, and say to them I wish and pray them all to seek to be Christians if they wish to be happy in this or the world to come.

Virgil is hurrying, so I can write no more.

T. BROWN

67

P.S. Sarah and A., write. I sympathize with you, Sarah, in the loss of your dear mother.

Alvin, I have forwarded your Grandpa's likeness to you and Sarah. I cut it from his volume of sermons.

Mary says kiss the children for her.

With love in her heart for God and neighbor, she was relaxed, was imparting hope to others, and still planning for the future. But in a few more weeks Mrs. Brown had gone to her reward.

Many years ago in Maryland she had written that she would be hoping to see her husband and her sweet little boy in the next world. This was in those early days in Maryland when Tabitha, with a wave of loneliness sweeping over her after watching the sun rising to begin another day, wrote: "I often bewail my sad fate. I weep, but weep alone till Aurora smilingly glides the east, extending her rays across the Virginia shore. She bids me dry my tears and weep no more." (It may be noted this is the only time we have the least hint of her having given way to tears.)

Then with her usual poise she continued, "Hope cheers the thinking mind. Thus, when our godly friends are summoned away our greatest cause of mourning is that we are deprived of the society we once delighted in."

She then added, "Though my afflictions have been of the most distressing nature, submission is my duty. . . . I do not expect to return to New England to spend my life, as we had intended to stay in Maryland, being surrounded by friends. . . . It matters but little what spot is allotted to us in this world. Our pilgrimage is short. Time is constantly on the wing. . . . I do not wish to change the decisions of the Almighty. He is merciful to those who put their trust in Him. I am resolved thus to be confident that whatsoever He suffers to take place, though grievous at first, will terminate for the best." (Selections from letter of June 24, 1817)

NOTE: The above letter was written to her husband's brother, Noyes Brown of Stonington, Connecticut.

Then after many years, and as an Oregon pioneer, Mrs. Brown in her far west home, still confident and radiant, declared, "I am a stranger to homesickness, for I carry my home with me wherever I go."

Pherne Brown Pringle to Kate Pringle Miller

June 1, 1869
Salem

MY DEAR GRANDDAUGHTER:

You have a task to rule with judgment and discretion, and maintain your place as a teacher should, for to learn, they must love their teacher.

I wish you could see the flowers, thirty or forty kinds of roses. . . .

September 11, 1888

I will picture a home made pleasant by a happy mother and her loving husband and her lovely children the Lord has given her to train for Him . . . for a brief moment. I ask the Lord to bless with his choicest blessings you and yours. He hears and knows our thoughts, and we are glad. . . .

Christmas Eve

I have but the use of one eye, but I am happy to know that I have friends who love me. The days are short and I enjoy them. . . .

January 25, 1889

. . . I think you choose the path of wisdom. You have a family of nice children that need all your care and attention. Live happily with them and love will follow. Teach them that God rules over all and will protect and care for them in every trouble,

69

in every place, and in amusements. . . . It is a pleasant road to travel. . . . Be thankful and have no misgivings. . . .

In all my letters, I think maybe this is my last . . . my thoughts run on . . . when our short life has run its length, and we are only waiting the summons to go.

I have a nice, large room, my bed, lounge, bureau, rocking chair, three other chairs, a large looking-glass, besides my drawings in frames hung around the room. There are three porches. I have all the earthly comforts I could enjoy, and good neighbors —a score of them. They will do anything for me. I love them all. Please write soon, dear Kate.

P. T. PRINGLE

April 25

. . . The man who is unmindful of flowers is unmindful of the love of God. Everything says, "Worship God." . . . The world with all its care and trials will not take from us this happiness. . . . Is it death, as we call it? No, no, it is life, life, to live forever.

The Lord will bless you and yours.

A mother's love to her son, PHERNE T. PRINGLE

(Earlier, Mrs. Pringle had mentioned that her son Clark Pringle was living on the other side of the Cascade Mountains. "There is halfway between us a great, white mountain covered summer and winter with a mantle of snow which I can see every time I look out to the east of us.")

Mrs. Pringle passed on the next month, May 21, 1891, aged 86 years.

This granddaughter Mrs. Kate Virgilia Pringle Miller had married James H. B. Miller, a brother of Joaquin Miller, the Poet of the Sierras.

It is noteworthy that Tabitha Brown reached the age of seventy-eight, her son Orus nearly seventy-four, her son Manthano seventy-three, and her daughter Pherne eighty-six.

Among her grandchildren, Alvin Clark was eighty-three, Andrew Orus seventy-five, Pherne Bain Strong eighty-two, Matthew seventy-nine, Rebecca seventy-four, Thomas Clark eighty-two, Rachel seventy-eight, Matilda nearly ninety, Tabitha Ella eighty-six, and Henrietta eighty-two.

Some of her descendants in the present generation are now past eighty.

The Story of Catherine Sager

(*Mrs. Clark Pringle*)

HENRY SAGER AND FAMILY started early in '44 to Oregon. Near the Rocky Mountains both Mr. and Mrs. Sager succumbed to illness. Then the captain of the train took their children to the mission at Walla Walla, Washington.

Dr. and Mrs. Marcus Whitman in company with three others had crossed the plains in 1836, ten years ahead of Tabitha Brown, Narcissa Whitman being the first white woman to cross the Rockies. At Walla Walla they had established their mission for Indian children.

On arrival at Whitman mission, Captain Shaw of the wagon train persuaded Dr. Whitman to take charge of the orphans, as several families were stopping over till spring. Dr. Whitman hesitated; he was employed by the Mission Board to teach and care for Indian children. He would have to draw on supplies apportioned for the mission school, which might bring censure from the Board. But orphans ranging in age from one to fifteen years were such an appeal that he could not bear to refuse. He said, "Let the censure come, if the Board should feel thet way." (Their own little girl had been drowned in Walla Walla River.)

After talking with John, the eldest, Dr. Whitman went to Oregon City, the capital of the Territory, and was appointed guardian of the Sager children. For three years they lived happily at the mission.

The Whitmans strictly observed the customs of civilization in

71

having worship services on Sunday. A day school was kept, hiring a teacher from among the emigrants staying over. It is said there were six hundred Indian children-who were pupils. In summer Mrs. Whitman taught them. She said, "We do not want to degenerate; instead, we want to draw them up."

The Indians were prospering. They had herds of horses and cattle; they learned to plant and raise some crops; they did not depend on hunting alone; and did not need to bring so many pelts to the fur traders. Nevertheless, some became dissatisfied.

In the meantime, the Hudson Bay Company had not encouraged emigration from the States to the Northwest, and much of the Louisiana Purchase country was still unknown. Dr. Whitman had convinced the United States government that the Northwest could be settled by emigrants traveling across the plains, and had demonstrated by conducting a train across in '43. This was the first train to take wagons overland to the Willamette Valley.

1847 was the fatal year when some of the emigrants brought in measles. The Indians were infected, and also the doctor's family. Due to the way the Indians were living, the disease was often fatal. It is said it was insinuated to the Indians that Dr. Whitman was poisoning them, although he had given them eleven years of his life.

The Whitmans, John and Frank Sager, and nine other men lost their lives, but the women and children were taken as prisoners.

It was greatly to the credit of Peter Skeen Ogden of the Hudson Bay Company that he came from Fort Vancouver bringing his own money and goods to Fort Walla Walla to negotiate with the Indians.

When delivered to Mr. Ogden, the prisoners had been there a month, since November 29, 1847. On New Year's Day '48 they started down the Columbia River in bateaux rowed by French voyageurs, and were taken to Oregon City to be given into the charge of the Territorial Governor. The orphans were then placed in homes.

Catherine Sager was taken into the home of Reverend William Roberts, supposedly in Portland, where she remained until she was grown. She married Clark Pringle, eldest son of Pherne Brown Pringle, and became the mother of Mrs. Kate Virgilia Pringle Miller.

As to Dr. Marcus Whitman, one may now venture the opinion that in his time he received scant recognition for several kinds of service rendered . . . besides the supreme sacrifice at the age of forty-five years.

To the Bluejay

I'm sorry your voice is so loud and so high.
I think folks dislike the harsh tones from your throat,
But you do stay quite late in the woodland nearby,
And God gave to you a nice, pretty blue coat.
—From Mountain to Shore

Tenderfoot Tales

And now this tale they do relate:
A Yank thought he'd go west;
He went from Maine to Jersey State,
And thought he'd been far west.

The tenderfoot thinks he'll have a ride:
The burro's slow as time—
It bites or kicks or jumps aside;
The boy will walk next time.
—From Mountain to Shore

What a Meal!

Just now I see a billboard high
All covered with a circus picture.
Two burros come and stand near by
And eat the tiger—what a mixture!
—*From Mountain to Shore*

Semi-Centennial of Pacific University

AFTER FIFTY YEARS . . .

THE FIRST GRADUATE of Pacific University was Harvey W. Scott, for many years editor of the *Portland Oregonian* and widely quoted across the country. His daughter was a generous donor and patron of the school.

THE FIFTIETH ANNIVERSARY

July 10, 1898
Sunday Oregonian, Portland

The semi-centennial of Tualatin Academy and Pacific University was fitly celebrated at Forest Grove today. . . . Five hundred men and women, including nearly all the delegates to the Congregational National Council and a goodly number of Portland citizens, boarded a special train and sped to Forest Grove . . . the peaks of the Cascade Range . . . Hood's head was pillowed on a bank of cumulus clouds . . . the dark green of timbered slopes. The brimming Willamette . . . wild flowers, yellowing grain, and ripening fruit . . . oaks and firs on the spacious

74

campus. Long tables in the shade, a thousand people, and none went hungry.

By Professor William Ferrin: The spirit and purpose which actuated the Puritans in founding Harvard and Yale, and their descendants who established Dartmouth and Williams, continued to possess their descendants as they migrated across the continent . . . along the northern belt of our country . . . its progress was marked by the founding of colleges, like the altars the patriarchs set up in Canaan to mark their progress through the Promised Land. Such an institution, founded in such a spirit, by such men and women is Pacific University. . . . The first of these is Mrs. Tabitha Moffatt Brown, a widow and nearly three-score-and-ten. With no family cares pressing upon her, but with the love of God and humanity in her heart, she cast about her for some work she could do. She became "Grandma Brown" to all the Willamette Valley. She was nurse to all the neighbors far and wide. Like that other Tabitha of St. Paul's time, she was "full of good works and alms deeds which she did." She found the work for which she is best known in these parts and, fifty-one years ago, she decided to open a school and home for orphan children of pioneers. . . . Early in the next year, the number of homeless waifs depending on Mrs. Brown increased through the exodus of men to the gold mines in California. Larger quarters were secured by the erection of a house of somewhat pretentious proportions by people who had become interested in the work of the orphanage.

Under the benevolent influence of a Rockefeller or a Leland Stanford, great universities have sprung up in a single night. They have come into existence full grown and well equipped. Not such has been the history of most of the colleges that have had the largest part in molding our national character. They began in a small way. Few colleges were more advanced at their jubilee than is Pacific today. Yale and Harvard were insignificant with the slenderest of endowments. Williams had three professors and two tutors. When Bowdoin was fifty years old, there were seven professors. . . . Near the platform hung the picture of "Grandma" Tabitha Brown.

75

Associated with Mrs. Brown in the work of the orphanage and actively cooperating was Reverend Harvey Clark. . . . He donated two hundred acres of his land as a foundation fund, and later another large tract. This land was then laid out and the proceeds from the sale helped to maintain the Academy and the College in their earlier years. Mr. Clark's gift involved the formation of no syndicate. It was a gift outright without any conditions whatever. From it he derived not one dollar. No town lots were reserved, the proceeds of whose sale would go into his own pocket. He is spoken of by men who knew him as peculiarly unselfish. Not a few colleges based upon syndicate would have been spared disaster if such disinterested generosity had characterized the founders.

Mrs. Brown had given up the idea of going east for funds but, after her passing, President Marsh went three times, raising $20,000 each time, securing additional teachers, and 5,000 volumes for the library. The school was set upon what was then considered a firm foundation.

—By special permission of the *Portland Oregonian*

Clark Brown's Address

March 31, 1795

IF ONLY MRS. BROWN's devoted husband could have seen that day at the semi-centennial of Pacific University when she was being honored! He, himself, was much interested in the establishment of schools. He once wrote that without education life would be insipid. The following paragraphs are now selected from an address he gave. (The full text is quite long, as in his day an address or sermon was expected on nearly every occasion, and none of them were short!)

Many who have been raised to stations of honor and usefulness have been taken from the most humble situations. A striking instance of this was shown in the life of Moses—Moses in the marshy weeds and Moses the Commander of the people and armies of the Lord of Hosts . . . standing upon the banks of the Red Sea safely conducting the chosen of the Lord through the paths of the watery element.

Whence was this strange, surprising reverse of fortune? Was it wholly owing to his being taken from the bulrushes? No. For notwithstanding he was thus saved, yet his eminence and worth are to be attributed to some greater cause. It was his education under the superintending providence of God which prepared him to be such a pattern of meekness, such a blessing to the chosen of the Lord. . . . Had it not been for his education, his genius, meekness, and virtue would, like a lump of unwrought gold, never have appeared according to their true value, but would have been concealed by the impenetrable shades of ignorance.

The education of children is an interesting concern to all those that are possessed of sentiments of love and compassion for them; as also to all such as have any regard for the well-being of mankind, especially of the communities to which they belong.

Should, therefore, the education of children become generally neglected, superstition, misery, and destruction would be the awful consequence. Intellectual pleasures, or those of a mind refined by celestial virtue and illuminated by the emanating rays of divine love, could then never expand in all their purifying and pleasurable effects. But few other joys and pleasures would be known, but those which are sensual, proceeding from hearts defiled like contaminated streams issuing from impure fountains. The honor of obtaining a victory over their own passions would be unknown, and the joys of a happy triumph over the powers of darkness' never possess their hearts. . . .

According as children are educated would be their notions, ideas, and practices when they shall come forth upon the theater of time. . . .

The real worth and superiority of mankind above the beasts of the forest appear only when cultivating and replenishing the mind with knowledge received from learning. . . . Learning not only capacitates the mind for scanning with pleasure the work and beauties of creation, but renders it a fit repository for consistent ideas of God, the great Creator and Upholder of all things.

Those minds which remain deformed have very inconsistent ideas of God, His perfections, and His dealings with His intelligent creatures. To the truth of this assertion, both history and our own observations will bear testimony. . . .

It is knowledge that teaches us to assert the sovereignty of our nature and to assume that dignity in the scale of being for which we were created. Thousands of utilities, joys, and pleasures owe their birth and being to it. By a certain progression, the mind learns for each of its ideas names with their use and design . . . ideas of reflection useful respecting virtue and morality in which is included our duty both toward God and man, as well as our joy, peace, and happiness. This is the way and manner with which the mind is furnished with ideas and the use of language; and by which it is enabled to exercise its discursive faculties. It, therefore, depends upon the right education of children respecting their future prosperity.

The divine portion of genius is diffused among the rich and the poor, the high, and the low, and needs only the polishing hand of education to make it shine in each with distinguished lustre.

The great disparity in mankind is not so much from the want of gifts, but from the want of proper education. Among crowds of the untutored real evidences of a bright genius may plainly be discovered. Many of those who traverse the American deserts to whom no other joys and pleasures are known but "the chase and the pipe" have as great if not greater natural abilities than those who among the civilized fill distinguished stations of usefulness and honor.

NOTE: Brown evidently had in mind the proverb, "Train up a child in the way he should go, and when he is old he will not depart from it," for he wrote, "Reason answers (after no fault of the proverb itself): 'Train up children in that way in which they will make valuable members of a community.' "

"And ye fathers, provoke not your children to wrath, but bring them up in the nurture and admiration of the Lord."

"This is the language of the Gospel: 'Seek ye first the Kingdom of God and His righteousness and all these things shall be added unto you!'"

It may be that the above address was the best known of Mr. Brown's published writings, as quite a number of original copies were located by this recorder. As mentioned elsewhere, there is on the outside cover the following from Deuteronomy: "Thou shalt teach them diligently unto thy children, and thou shalt talk of them when thou sittest in thine house, and when thou walkest by the Way, and when thou liest down and when thou risest up."

It was in the above address that he quoted:

> Perhaps in this neglected spot is laid
> Some heart once pregnant with celestial fire;
> Hands that the rod of empire might have sway'd
> Or wak'd to ecstasy the living lyre.

Our Idea of a Hero—1916

EDITORIAL ON DR. ELMER BROWN

DR. E. M. BROWN, whose passing yesterday cast a shadow of pain and sorrow over Tacoma, was perhaps the greatest living exponent of the Golden Rule this city has ever known. His every deed, so far as we ever have heard, was of kindness and charity.

The physician suffered inconceivable torture during the last dozen years of his life. A malady which he contracted in the Philippines, when he gave the best part of his life to his country, developed into a disease which science could not cure. Yet through it all he moved on serenely, giving cheer to those other sufferers whom he was called upon to aid; giving the best of his extensive surgical and medical knowledge to relieve others who lived in a world of pain; always smiling, always charitable and pleasant, even though his every day was one of misery.

Dr. Brown gave his services willingly to the poor. There are innumerable cases where his sympathy for the circumstances of his patients would not allow him to accept one penny for his labors. Had he received fees commensurate with his surgical ability, he would have become wealthy. But his charity, his love for humanity, and his simple Golden Rule creed caused him to remain comparatively poor.

Tacoma will always cherish the memory of one of its greatest citizens, Dr. E. M. Brown. It is said that the funeral of Dr. Brown was held in the largest hall in the city—the Armory. The Bar Association and the Medical Society attended in a body. Flags were at half-mast and, according to one account, stores were closed. (He was a son of Alvin Clark Brown.)

—By permission of Tacoma *News Tribune*

Wild Clematis Out West

On a zigzag fence of split rails made
By early settlers going there,
The clematis climbs far from the shade
Along the edge of a highway near.

With light, cream-colored flowers glowing
And finely-cut green leaves that cling,
These sturdy vines make quite a showing
Against the old, bare, brown railing.

And when the petals have lived and gone
These blossoms still are white and alluring—
Soft, shiny strands of silks live on
And cling in clusters late enduring.

—*From Mountain to Shore*

80

April

Showers are here and green blades, too;
Gulls are ever on the wing;
Though the sky's not always blue,
Each day is a part of spring.
Joy and I need never part
If 'tis April in my heart.

—*From Mountain to Shore*

A Tenderfoot Tale

A native takes a new-found friend
Up high to see a gorgeous view,
But where they reach a certain bend,
The only scene's on a billboard new.

—*From Mountain to Shore*

The Amazing Tabitha Brown

IT WAS HAZARDOUS AT BEST to cross the plains in the early days even when following the favorite routes. Nevertheless, the adventurous ones were still going along as before, the first train to Oregon having made the journey in 1830. One is left to various conjectures and may as well turn away from the subject.

Mrs. Brown referred years later only to the "vicissitudes" through which she had passed. It is obvious that she had the will to live, being well-bolstered by a keen sense of humor.

81

In estimating distinctive traits, one aspect may seem unimportant, yet to another person it may be highly interesting.

We may ponder words of wisdom from the honored Francis Bacon: "It is good in discourse to vary and intermingle the present occasion with arguments, tales with reasons, questions, telling of opinions, and jest with earnest."

"Grandma Brown," as she was known, was resourceful. Instead of frittering away her time on things of little or no consequence, she seemed to hold in reserve a certain strength for emergencies. This served her very well until that last summertime when she surely went beyond the limit and lived only a few months longer. She went on horseback through the mountains, camping out at the age of seventy-seven.

Though her sons sometimes considered her as being much too stern and severe, that seemingly stemmed from those early days when they had differed on the question of going to sea.

Although it makes the world seem brighter to accent only the pleasing tones, this scribe is not endeavoring to portray a character that did not exist, a sort of superwoman who was already twanging the strings of her heavenly harp while sauntering along the streets of gold. One reason? Her frank comments on youngsters in family letters are much better when deleted.

However, knowing her deep compassion and the pleasure she found in helping the orphans, we must freely give her credit. Instead of a jeremiad of the past, she was still singing a song of hope and the joy of living.

She was very versatile. Though poetic and artistic, she could suddenly turn to the most prosaic things and be absorbed in them.

And was she thrifty? The answer is always "Yes" . . . even if one did not happen to know that some of her father's forebears came from Scotland. It is known that when they started across the country Captain John Brown was wearing a moneybelt well filled with coins of gold; and that Tabitha had funds in reserve; but on arriving in Salem and seeing others in their party so needy, they gave away most of their money to those who had faced death with them so many days. (Incidentally, the

American Red Cross was then three or four years in the future.)
Obviously, Tabitha and Captain John both believed that steward-
ship includes even those who are "Scotch."

We may well surmise that little Miss Tabitha, aged seven,
had already heard Franklin's maxims quoted in Brimfield, as
Poor Richard's Almanac was widely distributed in Old New
England, that home of thrift and economy. Probably the *Almanac*
was in the Moffatt house; so we may suppose that in those young,
impressionable years she was familiar with: "Many a little makes
a mickle (or muckle)." . . . "A word to the wise is enough."
. . . "Always taking meal out of the tub and never putting meal
in soon comes to the bottom." "Wise men learn by others' harms."

Moreover, that was in 1797 when Franklin was busy arguing with the Convention members and trying to prevent them
from disbanding and leaving without writing the Constitution
(which seems to have a familiar sound).

It is noticeable that Franklin admitted, "To encourage the
practice of remembering those wise sentences, I have sometimes
quoted myself with great gravity."

Returning again to Mrs. Brown: As to the foregoing con-
siderations, methinks she would have approved Franklin's way
of putting first things first. We see this in her ideas of simple
needs and simple living. She was very much in the world, yet,
in a sense, was not of it. At one time she declared that she
intended to live well on her own choice bits of muckamuck
(food). But of this we may be certain: She never made unto
herself a god of any material thing, or bowed down and wor-
shipped it. Nor did she go into superlatives over some trifle;
she had seen enough of tragedy to evaluate such things.

There have been errors and misunderstandings, which is
natural. It is noticeable that in Oregon she walked with only
a slight limp due to a badly set legbone after a recent accident
on the "trek." According to the family, she was not helpless on
horseback, nor did she have to be lifted up to the saddle. Tabitha,
herself, wrote that it was Uncle John's cane in her hand, and
she had thrust it hard into the ground for him to pull himself up.

Also, she did not like dismounting, as she was riding a horse never before ridden by a woman. The strange flapping of a long dress had sometimes caused a horse to bolt and run away with the rider.

Nor had she ever "kept house" for Uncle John: In the East when he was not at sea, or staying in New York City, he was with Clark and Tabitha in their own home; in St. Charles he had purchased a house and had urged the Pringles when they were newly married to make a home for him, which they did; in Salem he still lived in the Pringles' home but had gone to Virgilia's house, where he suddenly died.

It is true that on arriving in Salem in an emergency situation, Tabitha had taken charge of the minister's house and children in return for his taking them—herself and Uncle John—into his home. But she tells of spending the following summer at the seashore and of getting settled at Forest Grove for the second winter, before opening her school in the spring of '48. Also, she began her school in the old log meetinghouse; the new building came later—not on condition that she could start the school.

One thing is sure: Descendants have never thought of her as a cripple. *Im Gegenteil und zum Beispiel,* she was "on call," so to speak, for the sick and needy for miles about the countryside.

Obviously, it was impossible that Orus could have warned his mother that she would be eight or nine months on the way, and so was trying to persuade her not to go. Tabitha, herself, wrote that it was a false guide acting as decoy who deserted them, leaving them to wander through several states, even sometimes chopping their way through forest to make a path for their wagons. (Orus had made the trip in three months by the regular trail, and had bitterly opposed their risking a suggested cut-off.) One cannot even estimate the number of wagons at a given time, as they were divided into different groups; for instance, when there was a choice of fords, some had shallow places and went ahead, while others had to wait some time for high water to go down, or for escaping cattle.

Several aspects of the ways of Mrs. Brown seem reminiscent of Clark when he wrote of President Washington, "He had the

84

applause of a good conscience." This doubtless increased her self-confidence.

It appears that when she came to an impasse, she managed to find a way out of that dead-end street. The clouds that rose near Mount Hood's snow and then came sailing overhead usually showed their silver linings when Mrs. Brown was present.

This is the strong-willed woman who could comment casually that she had been in an open boat thirteen days with the wind against them. Was Captain Brown there with practiced and skillful hand on the sail or sails? Did they have sufficient supplies? Was she ever tossed into the water and had to be fished out? Anyway, what an experience! It seems she was dedicated and inspired. Instead of pursuing happiness, she allowed it to come to her when she was busy lending a hand. Wherever she went she was held in high esteem.

It does seem well to have a standard to be held before our eyes, although we may never achieve it. . . . The pattern stands.

Solomon has offered this: "She seeketh wool and flax and worketh willingly with her hands. She riseth also while it is yet night and giveth meat to her household. She layeth her hands to the spindle, and her hands hold the distaff. She maketh coverings of tapestry. She maketh fine linen and selleth it; and delivereth girdles unto the merchant. She looketh well to the ways of her household, and eateth not the bread of idleness. In her tongue is the law of kindnes, and she reacheth forth her hands to the needy."

On the Campus at Pacific University

MEMORIALS, I

IT HAS BEEN SAID repeatedly that North Dakota has Sacajeweah, the Indian girl who gave directions and instructions to Lewis and Clark; the state of Washington has Marcus and Narcissa Whitman at Walla Walla—Mrs. Whitman being the first white woman to cross the Rockies—but Oregon has Tabitha Brown.

When strolling on the campus of Pacific University, the visitor sees memorials of Mrs. Brown. A unique petrified stump with plaque has stood for many years on the site where Tabitha began her orphan school in the old log meetinghouse in 1848.

One sees the Tabitha Brown Hall, which is a union building with the college bookstore in the basement.

Of special interest is the Old Hall, the first building of the university, the one of which Mrs. Brown was so very proud. This is now the museum with Indian and pioneer relics on display. Among these are some items that belong to Tabitha Brown, and utensils used by her; also, a pair of wooden skates that belonged to Orus Brown. In a tall case stands a flag made by Mrs. Brown and her girls.

Recently Captain John Brown's old sea chest has been contributed to the Museum. It is said to have patches of leather fastened down with nails, and the hinges are gone. When the French released Uncle John from a prison in France, they returned this old sea chest and his valuable papers, including his logbook water-soaked and ruined.

(Tabitha Brown had possession of his papers, and at the end she destroyed them all. In a note to Mrs. Pringle at Salem, she mentioned, "Do as you like with that fine linen shirt.")

If only the old chest could speak what stories it could tell! . . . Thomas Carlyle has reminded us how magically bright does many a little *reality* dwell in our remembrance . . . need only that the scene lie on this old firm Earth . . . that the personages be men . . . how some slight incident, if *real* and well presented, will fix itself in memory and lie ennobled there, silvered over with the pale cast of thought.

Then, too, there are Bibles, some of her husband's published sermons, letters, and newspapers. Among items contributed by descendants are a candle mold, a tea canister, a little porcelain cup, a music book and a spelling book. (It is probable that when Mrs. Brown's prairie schooner was wrecked in a rocky canyon, that a trunk had been transferred to one of Mr. Pringle's wagons.) Some heirloom jewelry belonging to Tabitha and given to her daughter Pherne was destroyed by fire when the Pringle house in Salem was burned in an early day.

There is another reminiscence of Great-grandmother Brown: She had sometimes admired a giant oak entwined in vines and standing on the campus. It was called the Tabitha Brown Tree, as she had in a lighthearted way commented when it was splintered by lightning that the tree, like her, had been crippled (meaning that she walked with a slight limp due to the broken and badly set legbone). Soon a swarm of bees from the nearby land of Alvin Clark Brown had moved into the hollow trunk of the tree, and had set up housekeeping operations. It was then also known as "old bee tree." Now comes word that on the insistence of a fire inspector the well-known tree has been taken away, but tourists and other visitors are still being told the story of the giant oak that was one of the pioneers.

We know that Mrs. Brown had always adored trees. In reading these lines this recorder is reminded of Bacon's advice to fill the mind with wonder and admiration, fables, stories, histories, and contemplations of nature. Doubtless Mrs. Brown would have agreed. Her own pathetic lines to the Butternut Tree are in tune with this, and also with Longfellow, Bryant, Thoreau, and other tree enthusiasts.

Today we may well wonder if prehistoric ancestors were of the genus *Druidaeus* of the order *Arboraceae* in their zealous worship of the sacred oak. If so, many of us today may be throwbacks in our roles as little twigs on the family tree! But let us exchange an oak for a maple. Then, whether it be woods, woodland, forest, green grove, or shady glen, let us joyfully enter and scan the wonders of Nature and Nature's God.

The Good Ship *Tabitha Brown*

MEMORIALS, II

THE SCENE is in a Portland shipyard. Friends and relatives have arrived—one, at least, having come from as far as Chicago—to witness the launching of a Liberty ship. The group is one of the largest ever to attend a ceremony of launching. Decorations of flags and flowers have all been arranged. Now there is music followed by a brief address and a prayer. There is a solo and a selection by a quartet. This is all very impressive in the tense atmosphere—a scene never to be forgotten.

Some of the hearers are deeply moved by the singing of "The Star Spangled Banner," as the author of the words, Francis Scott Key, was a family friend of the Clark Browns. There are some misty, tear-dimmed eyes. (Mr. Key, himself, had assembled some of the Clark Brown sermons after the passing of Mr. Brown and had published them in a separate volume, 1819.)

Soon the Liberty ship *Tabitha Brown* is launched. The time is October 16, 1942. Some two weeks later, November 2, 1942, she begins her long tour to distant seas. She is carrying a cargo of flour—flour for the aid of our Allies—and she is going around the world.

(There is another strange coincidence: It appears this is the second Liberty ship named after a woman, the first having been named for Anne Marbury Hutchinson, an ancestor of Tabitha Brown's husband. That ship was broken in two in a storm off the coast of Africa, but true to the Hutchinson pattern it surprisingly kept afloat even after being torpedoed two or three times. It was then towed into a harbor to be dismantled.)

Again as to the *Tabitha Brown*: It may be added that Wendell Brown, student at Pacific University, son of Ernest Clark Brown, grandson of Alvin Clark Brown, and great-grandson of Orus Brown, wrote:

I had a pleasant evening with one of the men who made the initial voyage on the *S.S. Tabitha Brown.*

The trip lasted almost six months, the ship circling the world, making stops in the South Pacific and many South American ports. While in the South Atlantic, thirteen of twenty-seven vessels were lost, but the *Tabitha* always escaped. The man brought home some souvenirs, including a picture of the gun crew of the *Tabitha.* They had witnessed many exciting adventures in the convoy.

It may be added that Wendell Brown gave his life in the Medical Corps, having succumbed to illness while being pushed through a shortened preparatory course. Later, there were reports that the *Tabitha* was seen in the Mediterranean bearing several marks on the smokestack.

If only Great-grandmother could have seen the sailing of those two ships! But perchance she did. . . . Who knows? ("The cloud of witnesses" . . .)

The Same Species Up North

THESE FEW SKETCHES of the Upper Peninsula are typical of the scenes and surroundings in New England where the Clark Browns lived. They had nearly the same species of trees, wild flowers and berries; there were the beaches and rocky shores, even sometimes including the fogs and the sea gulls. This was especially true of Maine and Massachusetts.

One may unconsciously think of the Northwoods as a band or belt extending from Nova Scotia to British Columbia, with abundant rainfall and usually lush vegetation, but what a gap across the plains!

In this Hiawathaland of ours, within the snowcap for several months, we have just south of here the "footprints" of Hiawatha and Laughing Water returning home from Minnehaha to the shores of Big Seawater. It all seems very real. Mrs. Brown would have enjoyed it all.

> With needles silky soft so like the pine endowed,
> But for a time, the tamarack in marsh kneedeep
> Shall not like fragrant fir and balsam be allowed
> Its summer store of shiny, shimmering green to keep.
> —*This Broad Land*

The main differences seem to be that Oregon has the giant holly being shipped in immense wreaths to distant places, and there is the extremely rare myrtle tree (said to be found also in the Holy Land).

We may note that in Tabitha's "explorations" she had missed only the deep South and the far Southwest . . . and that in the days of slow-motion travel.

Sea Gulls Against the Sky

> Just now a fishing tug is coming in,
> Its trail of smoke against the sky.
> Far out in Lake Superior it has been,
> Or in Iron Bay near by.
>
> Whatever language 'tis these creatures speak
> From Gull Rocks out to Granite Light,
> All seem to know the favorite food they seek
> Is drawing near; the boat's in sight.
>
> Five hundred gulls in circles soaring high,
> Excitedly they rush around,

Their graceful flight outlined against the sky,
A dome of brilliant blue background.

At eventide the bounteous feast is o'er,
The fish boats tied up near the docks,
And the gulls return along the curving shore,
To their chosen homes among the rocks.
                              —*This Broad Land*

I'd Like to Be a Worm

I'd like to be an angle worm
And with the angles live.
I'd only need to eat, keep warm;
No thought to war I'd give.

I'd not be bothered by inflation,
Or price of wheat and corn,
Nor worry over state and nation,
Nor wish I'd not been born.

On second thought, a bird might come
And eat me for his meal,
Or angler dig an early worm;
That might be no square deal.

I'd better be content as I am,
My daily problems meet,
And now decide 'twixt beef and lamb,
Corn flakes and shredded wheat.
                              —*This Broad Land*

91

From Far Maine to Minnehaha

(Selections from *Lines to Longfellow*)

We can ponder o'er your words now,
Join in love of forest with you.
You saw beauty in the pine tree,
In the cedar and the hemlock;
You saw shimmering lines of aspen
And spruce-tip upon the skyline,
Spruce grove striped with white of birch bole. . . .
You saw wonders in the simple,
You showed forth your love of nature,
Seeing beauty in the woodland,
Shading maidenhair and rue leaves,
Shading fresh fern fronds unrolling,
Sheltering varicolored violets
Growing near the white of trilliums;
Or the showy lady-slippers
And more pale and modest orchids
With the nearby green of mosses.
You heard music in the forest
From the feathered folk around you,
In the song in fall of river,
In the tinkle of the brooklet,
And the whisper in the pine bough. . . .
Folk can now to you be grateful
For the tales of wondrous valor—
Tales of courage of the hunter,
Mayhap with the flesh of bison,
In canoe along the lake shore,
From the distant hunt returning;
Tales of skillful hand of boatman

In the power of Gitche Gumee;
Tales of fortitude of women
And the patience in their labor
In primeval forest living,
Whether fashioning of deerskin,
Whether roasting of the deer meat,
Whether gathering herb for healing,
Or in gathering dry the driftwood,
Or in weaving of small willow,
Or in braiding of sweet-grass mat.
Folk can better understand now,
For you made the telling vivid,
Made the ancient ones seem living.
You interpreted the customs
Of both young and old together,
Asking Manitou for blessings
On the shores of "Big-Sea-Water."
Folk remember Old Nokomis
And the happy Laughing Water . . .
By small lake or maple forest,
With the fresh green moss on tree bole,
Or by shore of "Big-Sea-Water"
Near the rocks and dunes and beaches,
They who live among the north woods,
Seeing beauty all about them,
Honor oft your understanding
In your "stories and traditions
With the odors of the forest,
With the dew and damp of meadows."

—From Mountain to Shore

The Town That Was

Where buffalo grass waves its plumes in the breeze
And Indian paint brush stands by;
Where magpies go chattering through low pinion trees,
And seldom o'ercast is the sky;

Where yucca with daggers is piercing the air
And sharp, prickly pear needles grow;
Where primroses rise among rocks round and bare,
And white thistle-poppy blooms show;

Where water seethes hot from the side of a hill
Stands the last of a pioneer town.
But few are the ones who are living there still;
The houses are fast falling down.

I see the old depot once painted bright red,
And sidetrack where trains used to meet.
A tin cock is crowing with proud lifted head
On the roof of the well in the street.

There stands the hotel like a ghost dressed in brown,
Since the days when it sheltered great men,
And gay summer cottagers came to the town—
For the village was popular then;

And the cottonwood trees on both sides of the street,
The post-office sign on the door;
The crunching of gravel with slow-passing feet
By the old corner grocery store.

94

The little wood church is all weathered and gray,
Its small shingle roof sliding down,
A silent reminder of an earlier day
When summer folk came to the town.

The angler still comes to the same fishing place
With his reel and his rod and his fly;
And the river still roars like a rushing mill-race
In June when the water is high.

Those Good Old Days

(1899)

I went with Cousin on a shopping spree.
She took a quarter along;
A nickel bought Swiss steak for three.
(When liver was given for a song.)

A nickel bought small turnips white,
A nickel bought green things,
A fourth bought fruit for our delight
By well-known mineral springs.

The housewife returning made a cake
With icing pink piled high,
And fluffy potatoes she did make
Piled almost to the sky.

No motor overran the nation,
Just a horse or trolley was seen.
Nobody talked about inflation
And life was more serene.

—*From Mountain to Shore*

ODD LITTLE STORY

The first poem had been consigned to the wastebasket and forgotten some thirty years before; then rescued by husband and hidden in a bookcase. What a surprise when discovered barely in time for a volume of verse!

Give Us Hope

Melt, O slowly melt,
On sunny slopes, ye snow,
And give new hope of spring,
Give this before you go.

From cliff and rocky crag
And crevices within,
Pray take the mantle off
Where winter drifts have been.

Full many days in fall
'Mid wind and chilly blast
We watched your feathery flakes
And knew your hoard would last.

When winter's furious gale
With wild and doleful moan
Drove down the chimney place
In melancholy tone,

Each storm that passed this way
Still added flake to flake,
And drifts that higher grew
Were left within its wake.

But now since winter's days
Are spent and spring draws near,
The hope that always leads
Us on seems dear, seems dear.
            —*From Mountain to Shore*

We Follow the Scouts

(1928-29)

Now here I am in my West again
And drive where buffalo
Once grazed along the level plain
And braved the winter snow.

I'll leave to the past the tire that blew
Along a busy way,
And the big green caterpillar, too,
I sat upon that day.

My eyes can follow the meandering Platte
With its scanty fringe of trees,
For the land is open and the land is flat,
Appearing as elms, these trees,

Where the Indian came in his canoe
With fur for the trader to buy,
And scouts the easy fords well knew
When they were passing by.

Abruptly rising from the plain,
How strange the Black Hills land!
Where the scouts now seem to live again
And mementos there still stand.

I drive on through a castle gate
Past boulders towering high;
And leave the place where folks relate
Tall stories just as high.

The mountains first appearing dim
Soon better come in view,
And as I watch the sky's blue rim
They seem but a fainter hue.

To Codyland I'm on my way,
The home of Buffalo Bill,
With geyserland not far away
And Wild West stories still.

Stagecoach preserved and old ox-yoke
Kept since the days of yore,
Once far from the engine's puff of smoke,
Give much to ponder o'er.

Two buffalo heads that are hung high
Where a mountain goat stands near,
And an old Dutch oven now close by
Remind of the pioneer.

A cowboy's riding suit I see,
Packsaddle very old;
A pick and shovel, too, I see,
And a pan for washing gold.

Today I see a lone ranchhouse
With roof that's flat and square,
And many a mile from another house,
But a radio pole is there.

Now as I leave this northern place,
The land of the Yellowstone,

I find in a part of the far-flung space
That bountiful wheat is grown.

Sometimes dry farming's working well
And sometimes it is not.
The farmer has many tales to tell
About his chosen plot.

At seedtime when the gale is high
Before it sweeps the plain,
The farmer must stand idly by
While the wind blows out the grain.

I drive a lonely desert road
Where scarce a car I've found;
It's almost eve and in desert mode
There's stillness all around.

And now I reach old Medicine Bow,
Rich in Wild Western lore,
Where one roof only do I know
And not a dozen more.

I see a single column of smoke,
From a cottage a flickering light,
And soon, as if by a heavy cloak,
All's blotted out by night.

But, oh, this land of mystery
Where long-lost races trod,
With here and there but a trace to see,
Now covered o'er with sod.

*　　*　　*

A stretch of the Oregon Trail I find,
In Wyoming known to be,

Where wagon wheels had left behind
Cuts in soft marl I see.

Folk started on a springtime day
As others joined the train,
All eager for that land far away
Before snow could come again.

Then traveling first through old homeland,
They bade farewell each day
To kith and kin they left behind,
For they went west to stay.

Now some of these on horseback rode
Along an easy way;
Their limit was slow-moving mode
Of the oxen day by day.

Then as they made their camp for the night
With wagons in a ring,
The livestock grazed by late daylight,
And children played in the ring.

And then each morn with breakfast o'er,
The unwinding corral on its way,
And nearer their goal than e'er before,
They began another day.

At last the old Columbia Way,
And Portland, Salem, too,
With misty eyes some arrived that day
Where the hardy ones came through.

With forest dense and water near
By Willamette then they went
And soon had homes that they held dear
On the west of the continent.

Now as my path I'm following,
A glimpse of Mount Hood I see;
It pours its snow through falls that sing
Multnomah's melody.

With myriad pale-green pendants swinging,
The delicate hop vines climb;
To latticed trelliswork they're clinging
Like lace in summertime.

Today I see the pelicans
Take off from Klamath Lake;
Immense white planes they seem to be
When they a landing make.

I'll see where the frisky salmon leap,
And watch the waterfalls;
I'll ferry across each bay that's deep
And pass by cannery walls.

At Port Orford now I walk the beach
In quiet solitude;
When scarce a soul's within eye-reach,
Just Pacific's quiet mood.

There's nothing sordid here I see,
No heedless shove and push,
Just the heavens above and boundless sea
And over all a hush.

The Redwood Highway lures me now,
I'm southward bound today;
Almost with reverence I could bow
To these ancients by my way.

The City now I'm passing by,
On the Bay are beams of light

That seem to lean against the sky
On a moonless summer night.

I go where oranges are growing
And see large fig leaves green,
Ripe olives dark 'gainst pale leaves showing,
And vineyards in the scene.

If the '49 gold-rushers could
Just be upon this ground,
I think, as I am now, they would
Be surprised at all they'd found.

From a gulch a creek runs down today
Deep below the bridge I've crossed,
And through soft beach sand cuts its way
To the sea where it is lost.

At Santa Fe Spanish atmosphere
Reminds this age of men,
Of those first comers who settled here
And founded the city then.

We roll back pages of history,
Quaint town of the far Southwest,
And find much more that proved to be
To us of interest.

In a nearby town more atmosphere—
Red peppers on strings are swinging;
Reproductions of hammered silverware,
And early customs clinging.

I've seen the city of my birth,
A seemingly strange land;
But still it's on the same good earth
Near where my mountains stand.

I've followed the Arkansas' winding way
Between high canyon walls;
I've heard the roar and seen the spray
Of wildly dashing falls.

I'm going back to pin-cherry trees,
Huckleberries, and second growth,
For my love's divided twixt such as these
And pinions, but I love both.

So now I've come back home again
And want to think things o'er;
Up north I'll live it all again
And understand it more.

CPSIA information can be obtained at www.ICGtesting.com
Printed in the USA
LVOW01s0208020514

384022LV00007B/137/P